Essential Licensing Questions

Windows Server 2000 – 2012 R2

By
Louise Ulrick
Rich Gibbons

Published by Licensing School.

Copyright © 2016 Licensing School.

All rights reserved.

ISBN: 978-0-9931251-4-0.

No part of this publication may be reproduced, transmitted, or stored in or introduced into any information storage and retrieval system, in any form or by any means, electronic or mechanical, without permission in writing from Licensing School.

Introduction

GETTING THE MOST FROM THIS BOOK

This is a book of questions and answers and, as such, it's not designed to be read from start to finish. Use it whenever you've got a question on Windows Server that you need to find a quick and accurate answer to. While you will learn things about Windows Server that you didn't know before, its primary aim is not to be a teaching tool – we have other books that do a good job of that. The sections below give you an idea of the best way of using this book.

The Products

This book is about Windows Server, a product which is available in different editions and through different channels. We have focused on the licenses available through Microsoft's Volume Licensing agreements, but we've included a couple of questions on some of the OEM licenses where the answers took us by surprise. We've also chosen to focus on the licenses aimed at the larger business so we haven't included products such as Small Business Server and its friends. In terms of how far back we've gone with the detailed questions and answers – well, we went as far back as Windows Server 2008 since that version is still in extended support. For versions before that, we've opted to just include some key information that we thought would be useful.

The Questions

Finding the answer to your question is one thing, actually finding the question is another. You should use the Glossary in this book if you have a "what is...?" type of question – "What is the Processor-based/CAL licensing model?" for example. Otherwise, use the Index where we've grouped the questions into manageable chunks. For instance, you may be wondering whether an Enterprise Mobility Suite USL can be used instead of a CAL to access Windows Server 2012 R2. Just find the CALs section for Windows Server 2012 R2 and you'll find the answer amongst those questions on pages 11 and 12.

Introduction

The Answers
Our goal with the answers that we've provided is to give you explanations in normal English, rather than direct quotes from Microsoft's documents. If you want to review the original text from Microsoft then you can always turn to the reference that is part of every answer. This is also, of course, the reference you should use if you're documenting any licensing decisions that you've made.

You may come across one or two questions where you think the answer is very obvious and wonder why we've included them. You probably know already that you must never assume anything in licensing and so we've included these questions just to remove any doubt or guesswork!

The References
Some of Microsoft's most useful documents are the Product List, the Product Use Rights and, more recently, the Product Terms documents. These are the documents that we've taken the vast majority of our references from. Where we simply couldn't find proof of the answers we wanted in these documents then we've occasionally used Microsoft Volume Licensing Briefs or Licensing Guides. You'll find all of these on the Licensing School website at http://bit.ly/MSlicensingguides. Sometimes we wanted to include a definition which didn't appear anywhere and this is where you'll see "Licensing School" as the reference.

As far as possible we've used the documents where a particular version of Windows Server was last mentioned. So, for example, Windows Server 2012 last appeared in the October 2013 Product List and the July 2013 Product Use Rights, so those are the documents we've used. Just a note on these documents – we were using Word 2013 or later and therefore if documents opened in Compatibility Mode we let them. If you're using a different version of Word you may experience Compatibility Mode more or less frequently – and you may find that the references are one or two pages different.

Sometimes the documents were not so kind as to answer a specific question explicitly. For instance, are there down-edition rights for Windows Web Server 2008? Well, there aren't, but the Product Use Rights document doesn't state this. So, for our reference we've used the page range where it would have stated the down-edition rights if indeed they existed.

Errors
We try as hard as possible to make sure that there are no errors in our books but, recognizing that we are indeed only human, we promise that if you've bought one of our books we'll always let you know if an error should be discovered.

Keeping up to date
We all know that Microsoft's licensing changes at an astonishing pace – this book was produced in March 2016 and all information was accurate at the time of printing. In actual fact, the licensing rules for the individual products don't change much at all between different editions of the Product Terms and so this information is likely to remain accurate for the life of Windows Server 2012 R2 – and of course the information for the older versions won't change at all. If you want to know if we've released a later version of the book then the best way is to check our website at licensingschool.co.uk.

If you want to keep up to date with all aspects of Microsoft licensing then you'll find these resources useful:
- Subscribe to our blog and receive regular updates: blog.licensingschool.co.uk
- Sign up for our free fortnightly licensing newsletter: licensingschool.co.uk/register
- Keep in touch on social media – you'll find us on Twitter, LinkedIn and Facebook – just search for Licensing School

We're always interested in your feedback and you can get hold of us at info@licensingschool.co.uk if you'd like to.

Introduction

The Licensing School Team

It's very good fun working at Licensing School – we get to write cool books like this! We're a team that get on well together and writing a book is very much a team effort, so although it's Louise's and Rich's names on the front covers as the authors, the book couldn't have been completed without the other members of our team.

Simon Taylor, manager of the Licensing School Office, had the idea for the Glossary, and has spent hours proof reading and checking the hundreds of references in this book. You may also be familiar with some of Simon's other work – he's the creative brain behind all the fictional company names that we use in our licensing scenarios. So, if you love Cyan Ida's Pharmacy then that's down to him.

Paul Burgum, the Head Master of Licensing School, has endless patience as a sounding board for our (sometimes mad) ideas, and guides us and the business with integrity and compassion. His support in all our projects means that we enjoy what we do and can create resources like this.

And finally, the authors, whose voices you hear throughout this book. Louise Ulrick started life as a maths teacher in the UK, and thoroughly enjoys explaining licensing to people. This book was her original idea, and it's been rewarding for her seeing it come to life and being completed working alongside Rich.

Rich Gibbons is the newest member of the Licensing School staff and with his quirky sense of the ridiculous he's fitted in just fine! Rich is renowned for his shirts, his love of licensing, and once won a prize for a Windows 8 rap...

Windows Server: General Licensing Questions

WINDOWS SERVER
General Licensing Questions

CALs

1. **Can one organization use its Windows Server CALs to access another organization's Windows Servers?**
   No.

   Reference: page 70, March 2016 Product Terms.

2. **If an organization has multiple Windows Servers in their network are multiple Windows Server CALs required?**
   No. For example, if an organization had four Windows Servers, then a single CAL assigned to a user or device would allow access to any of the four Windows Servers.

   Reference: page 70, March 2016 Product Terms.

3. **Can Windows Server User and Device CALs be mixed in an organization's deployment of Windows Server?**
   Yes.

   Reference: page 70, March 2016 Product Terms.

4. **Through which Volume Licensing agreements can Windows Server CALs be purchased?**
   Windows Server CALs are available through these agreements:
   - Open
   - Open Value non-Company Wide
   - Select Plus
   - MPSA

   Windows Server CALs are not available through these agreements:
   - Open Value Subscription
   - Open Value Company Wide
   - Enterprise Agreement
   - Enterprise Subscription Agreement

   Reference: page 44, March 2016 Product Terms.

Windows Server: General Licensing Questions

5. **Can Windows Server User CALs be switched to Device CALs and vice versa?**
   Yes, but only when Software Assurance is renewed.

   Reference: page 74, March 2016 Product Terms.

6. **Can Windows Server CALs be used to allow concurrent usage, rather than being assigned to specific users or devices?**
   Yes, this is known as Per Server mode where CALs may be assigned to a specific Windows Server virtual machine or physical server to allow concurrent usage by users or devices.

   Reference: page 9, March 2016 Product Terms.

7. **Do Windows Server CALs allow access to earlier versions of Windows Server software?**
   Yes. For example, a Windows Server 2012 CAL allows access to a server licensed with Windows Server 2008 R2 Standard.

   Reference: page 70, March 2016 Product Terms.

External Connector License

8. **Does a Windows Server External Connector license allow access to earlier versions of Windows Server software?**
   Yes. For example, a Windows Server 2012 External Connector license allows access to a server licensed with Windows Server 2008 R2 Standard.

   Reference: page 70, March 2016 Product Terms.

9. **Is there a limit to the number of external users that can access a Windows Server licensed with a Windows Server External Connector license?**
   No.

   Reference: page 70, March 2016 Product Terms.

Software Assurance

10. **Can Software Assurance be added to a Windows Server license or to a CAL after the initial purchase?**
    No.
    Reference: page 73, March 2016 Product Terms.

11. **Which Software Assurance benefits are available for Windows Server?**
    - 24x7 Problem Resolution Support
    - Azure Hybrid Use Benefit
    - Disaster Recovery Rights (SA required for both Server licenses and CALs)
    - E-Learning
    - Extended HotFix Support
    - License Mobility across Server Farms (External Connector licenses only)
    - New Version Rights
    - Planning Services
    - Self-Hosting
    - Rights to purchase Step-Up licenses

    Reference: pages 46 & 74–75, March 2016 Product Terms.

12. **Can a new version of Windows Server be deployed after Software Assurance has expired?**
    Yes, if that new version was available while the Software Assurance was still active.
    Reference: page 75, March 2016 Product Terms.

Windows Server: General Licensing Questions

License Reassignment

13. **Can Windows Server licenses or CALs be reassigned?**

    Yes, although generally no more frequently than every 90 days. Exceptions occur when there is permanent hardware failure or termination of a user's employment, and CALs can be temporarily reassigned to cover a user's absence or the unavailability of a device that is out of service.

    Reference: page 6, March 2016 Product Terms.

Downgrade Rights

14. **If a license for one version of Windows Server is purchased, can an earlier version be deployed in its place?**

    Yes, an earlier version of the same edition can be deployed. So if a Windows Server 2012 R2 Standard license is purchased, Windows Server 2008 R2 Standard can be installed if required.

    Reference: page 6, March 2016 Product Terms.

15. **If one version of Windows Server is purchased but an older one is deployed, which product's licensing rules prevail?**

    The use rights of the version purchased (the licensed version), not the installed version, will always apply.

    Reference: page 6, March 2016 Product Terms.

Virtualization Licensing

16. **If a Windows Server virtual machine is not running, does it need to be licensed?**

    No, only virtual machines that are considered to be running need to be licensed, and a virtual machine is considered to be running until it is removed from memory.

    Reference: pages 9 & 71, March 2016 Product Terms.

Fail-Over Licensing

17. Which licenses are required for Windows Server running on a passive fail-over server?

Some Microsoft products include fail-over rights where a passive fail-over server may be run with no further licensing implications. This is NOT the case for Windows Server and a passive fail-over server must be licensed for Windows Server in the usual way.

Reference: pages 46 and 68, March 2016 Product Terms.

Storage Server

18. Is Windows Storage Server available through a Volume Licensing agreement?

No.

Reference: page 44, March 2016 Product Terms.

Windows Server 2012 R2

Windows Server 2012 R2

Date Available

19. **When was Windows Server 2012 R2 first available?**
    October 2013.

    Reference: page 44, March 2016 Product Terms.

Licenses

20. **What are the different licenses available for Windows Server 2012 R2?**
    - Windows Server 2012 R2 Standard license
    - Windows Server 2012 R2 Datacenter license
    - Windows Server 2012 CAL
    - Windows Server 2012 External Connector license

    Reference: page 44, March 2016 Product Terms.

Licensing Models

21. **How is Windows Server 2012 R2 Standard licensed?**
    With the Processor-based and CAL model.

    Reference: page 44, March 2016 Product Terms.

22. **How is Windows Server 2012 R2 Datacenter licensed?**
    With the Processor-based and CAL model.

    Reference: page 44, March 2016 Product Terms.

Windows Server 2012 R2

CALs

23. **Which licenses can be used to access Windows Server 2012 R2 Standard and Datacenter?**
    - Windows Server 2012 CAL
    - Enterprise Mobility Suite USL

    Alternatively, any of the following licenses can be used as long as they had active SA in August 2012 when Windows Server 2012 was first made available, or they were purchased after that date:
    - Core CAL Suite
    - Core CAL Suite Bridge for Office 365
    - Core CAL Suite Bridge for Intune
    - Core CAL Suite Bridge for Office 365 and Intune
    - Enterprise CAL Suite
    - Enterprise CAL Suite Bridge for Office 365
    - Enterprise CAL Suite Bridge for Intune
    - Enterprise CAL Suite Bridge for Office 365 and Intune

    Reference: pages 45 & 72, March 2016 Product Terms.

24. **Are Windows Server 2012 CALs used to access Windows Server 2012 R2?**
    Yes.

    Reference: page 45, March 2016 Product Terms.

25. **Are there Windows Server 2012 R2 CALs?**
    No, the Windows Server 2012 CALs were not updated when the Windows Server 2012 R2 licenses were released.

    Reference: page 44, March 2016 Product Terms.

26. **Can Windows Server 2012 CALs be used to access both Standard and Datacenter editions of Windows Server 2012 R2?**
    Yes.

    Reference: page 45, March 2016 Product Terms.

Windows Server 2012 R2

27. **Are Windows Server 2012 CALs available as both Device and User CALs?**
    Yes.
    Reference: page 25, October 2013 Product List.

28. **Are CALs required to access a Windows Server 2012 R2 physical environment that is used solely to host and manage virtual machines?**
    No.
    Reference: page 9, March 2016 Product Terms.

29. **If a server licensed for Windows Server 2012 R2 needs to access another licensed server, is a CAL required for the accessing server?**
    No.
    Reference: page 9, March 2016 Product Terms.

30. **Are CALs required if Windows Server 2012 R2 is being used for High Performance Computing?**
    No.
    Reference: page 9, March 2016 Product Terms.

31. **Are CALs required if Windows Server 2012 R2 is running a Web Workload?**
    No.
    Reference: page 9, March 2016 Product Terms.

Microsoft Identity Manager 2016

32. **Does a Windows Server 2012 CAL give access to Microsoft Identity Manager 2016?**
    No. While the server functionality is included in a Windows Server 2012 R2 Standard or Datacenter license, an additional Microsoft Identity Manager 2016 User CAL is required for all users accessing the Microsoft Identity Manager functionality.
    Reference: page 45, March 2016 Product Terms.

Per Server Mode

33. Can Windows Server 2012 R2 Standard be licensed in Per Server mode?
Yes.

Reference: page 9, March 2016 Product Terms.

34. Can Windows Server 2012 R2 Datacenter be licensed in Per Server mode?
Yes.

Reference: page 9, March 2016 Product Terms.

External Users

35. How are external users licensed for Windows Server 2012 R2 Standard?
- Windows Server 2012 CAL, or
- Windows Server 2012 External Connector license

Reference: page 45, March 2016 Product Terms.

36. How are external users licensed for Windows Server 2012 R2 Datacenter?
- Windows Server 2012 CAL, or
- Windows Server 2012 External Connector license

Reference: page 45, March 2016 Product Terms.

37. How is the Windows Server 2012 External Connector license used?
One Windows Server 2012 External Connector license must be assigned to each physical server accessed by external users. The server itself must be licensed in the usual way for Windows Server 2012 R2 using either Standard or Datacenter edition licenses.

Reference: page 70, March 2016 Product Terms.

Windows Server 2012 R2

38. Is there a Windows Server 2012 R2 External Connector license?

No, the Windows Server 2012 External Connector license was not updated when the Windows Server 2012 R2 licenses were released.

Reference: page 44, March 2016 Product Terms.

Virtualization Licensing

39. How is Windows Server 2012 R2 Standard licensed in a virtualized environment?

All physical processors on the server must be licensed with Processor-based licenses where one license covers up to two processors. Each license assigned to the physical server allows the running of Windows Server in up to two virtual machines. Additional licenses can be assigned to the server to allow two more virtual machines to be run per license. Windows Server can also be installed on the physical server, but in this case may only be used to manage the virtual machines.

Reference: page 9, March 2016 Product Terms.

40. How is Windows Server 2012 R2 Datacenter licensed in a virtualized environment?

All physical processors on the server must be licensed with Processor-based licenses, where one license covers up to two processors, and then unlimited virtual machines running Windows Server are allowed. Windows Server can also be installed on the physical server to run applications and/or to manage the virtual machines.

Reference: page 9, March 2016 Product Terms.

41. Can different editions of Windows Server 2012 R2 be run in the virtual machines on a single physical server?

Yes, as per the applicable downgrade/down-edition rights for the edition of Windows Server licensing the physical server.

Reference: page 6, March 2016 Product Terms.

Windows Server 2012 R2

42. **How is the Windows Server 2012 External Connector license used in a virtualized environment?**

    Each Windows Server 2012 External Connector license permits external users to access the physical server or any virtual machines running on that server.

    Reference: page 16, Volume Licensing Brief: "Licensing Microsoft server products for use in virtual environments" – April 2014.

Down-Edition Rights

43. **What are the down-edition rights for Windows Server 2012 R2 Standard?**

    Any earlier version of Windows Server in the following editions can be deployed:
    - Enterprise
    - Web Server
    - HPC Edition

    Reference: page 44, March 2016 Product Terms.

44. **What are the down-edition rights for Windows Server 2012 R2 Datacenter?**

    Any earlier version of Windows Server in the following editions can be deployed:
    - Standard
    - Enterprise
    - Web Server
    - HPC Edition

    Reference: page 44, March 2016 Product Terms.

Windows Server 2012 R2

License Mobility

45. Do any of the Windows Server 2012 R2 licenses have License Mobility?

None of the Windows Server 2012 R2 licenses have License Mobility through Software Assurance rights. A Windows Server 2012 External Connector license with active SA has License Mobility across Server Farms rights.

Reference: pages 46 & 82–83, March 2016 Product Terms.

Step-Up Licenses

46. Can a Windows Server 2012 R2 Standard license be stepped up to a Windows Server 2012 R2 Datacenter license?

Yes, with active SA.

Reference: page 81, March 2016 Product Terms.

Prior Versions

47. What is the prior version of Windows Server 2012 R2 Standard?

Windows Server 2012 Standard.

Reference: page 44, March 2016 Product Terms.

48. What is the prior version of Windows Server 2012 R2 Datacenter?

Windows Server 2012 Datacenter.

Reference: page 44, March 2016 Product Terms.

49. What is the prior version of the Windows Server 2012 External Connector license?

Windows Server 2008 External Connector license.

Reference: page 44, March 2016 Product Terms.

Windows Server 2012 R2

Mainstream and Extended Support Dates

50. When does mainstream support end for Windows Server 2012 R2 Standard and Datacenter editions?

January 9, 2018.

Reference: https://support.microsoft.com/en-us/lifecycle?p1=17383

51. When does extended support end for Windows Server 2012 R2 Standard and Datacenter editions?

January 10, 2023.

Reference: https://support.microsoft.com/en-us/lifecycle?p1=17383

Windows Server 2012

Date Available

52. **When was Windows Server 2012 first available?**
    August 2012.
    Reference: page 25, October 2013 Product List.

Licenses

53. **What are the different licenses available for Windows Server 2012?**
    - Windows Server 2012 Standard license
    - Windows Server 2012 Datacenter license
    - Windows Server 2012 CAL
    - Windows Server 2012 External Connector license

    Reference: page 25, October 2013 Product List.

Licensing Models

54. **How is Windows Server 2012 Standard licensed?**
    With the Processor-based and CAL model.
    Reference: page 25, July 2013 Product Use Rights.

55. **How is Windows Server 2012 Datacenter licensed?**
    With the Processor-based and CAL model.
    Reference: page 25, July 2013 Product Use Rights.

CALs

56. Which licenses can be used to access Windows Server 2012 Standard and Datacenter?
- Windows Server 2012 CAL

Alternatively, any of the following licenses can be used as long as they had active SA in August 2012 when Windows Server 2012 was first made available, or they were purchased after that date:
- Core CAL Suite
- Core CAL Suite Bridge for Office 365
- Core CAL Suite Bridge for Intune
- Core CAL Suite Bridge for Office 365 and Intune
- Enterprise CAL Suite
- Enterprise CAL Suite Bridge for Office 365
- Enterprise CAL Suite Bridge for Intune
- Enterprise CAL Suite Bridge for Office 365 and Intune

Reference: pages 26 & 27, July 2013 Product Use Rights.

57. Can Windows Server 2012 CALs be used to access both Standard and Datacenter editions of Windows Server 2012?
Yes.

Reference: page 25, October 2013 Product List.

58. Are Windows Server 2012 CALs available as both Device and User CALs?
Yes.

Reference: pages 26 & 27, July 2013 Product Use Rights.

59. Are CALs required to access a Windows Server 2012 physical environment that is used solely to host and manage virtual machines?
No.

Reference: page 25, July 2013 Product Use Rights.

Windows Server 2012

60. **If a server licensed for Windows Server 2012 needs to access another licensed server, is a CAL required for the accessing server?**
    No.

    Reference: page 25, July 2013 Product Use Rights.

61. **Are CALs required if Windows Server 2012 is being used for High Performance Computing?**
    No.

    Reference: page 183, October 2013 Product List.

62. **Are CALs required if Windows Server 2012 is running a Web Workload?**
    No.

    Reference: page 183, October 2013 Product List.

Per Server Mode

63. **Can Windows Server 2012 Standard be licensed in Per Server mode?**
    Yes.

    Reference: page 25, July 2013 Product Use Rights.

64. **Can Windows Server 2012 Datacenter be licensed in Per Server mode?**
    Yes.

    Reference: page 25, July 2013 Product Use Rights.

External Users

65. **How are external users licensed for Windows Server 2012 Standard?**
    - Windows Server 2012 CAL, or
    - Windows Server 2012 External Connector license

    Reference: page 27, July 2013 Product Use Rights.

Windows Server 2012

66. How are external users licensed for Windows Server 2012 Datacenter?
- Windows Server 2012 CAL, or
- Windows Server 2012 External Connector license

Reference: page 26, July 2013 Product Use Rights.

67. How is the Windows Server 2012 External Connector license used?

One Windows Server 2012 External Connector license must be assigned to each physical server accessed by external users. The server itself must be licensed in the usual way for Windows Server 2012 using either Standard or Datacenter edition licenses.

Reference: page 25, July 2013 Product Use Rights.

Virtualization Licensing

68. How is Windows Server 2012 Standard licensed in a virtualized environment?

All physical processors on the server must be licensed with Processor-based licenses where one license covers up to two processors. Each license assigned to the physical server allows the running of Windows Server in up to two virtual machines. Additional licenses can be assigned to the server to allow two more virtual machines to be run per license. Windows Server can also be installed on the physical server, but in this case may only be used to manage the virtual machines.

Reference: page 25, July 2013 Product Use Rights.

69. How is Windows Server 2012 Datacenter licensed in a virtualized environment?

All physical processors on the server must be licensed with Processor-based licenses, where one license covers up to two processors, and then unlimited virtual machines running Windows Server are allowed. Windows Server can also be installed on the physical server to run applications and/or to manage the virtual machines.

Reference: page 25, July 2013 Product Use Rights.

Windows Server 2012

70. **Can different editions of Windows Server 2012 be run in the virtual machines on a single physical server?**

    Yes, as per the applicable downgrade/down-edition rights for the edition of Windows Server licensing the physical server.

    Reference: pages 27 & 28, July 2013 Product Use Rights.

71. **How is the Windows Server 2012 External Connector license used in a virtualized environment?**

    Each Windows Server 2012 External Connector license permits external users to access the physical server or any virtual machines running on that server.

    Reference: page 16, Volume Licensing Brief: "Licensing Microsoft server products for use in virtual environments" – April 2014.

Down-Edition Rights

72. **What are the down-edition rights for Windows Server 2012 Standard?**

    Any earlier version of Windows Server in the following editions can be deployed:

    - Enterprise
    - Web Server
    - HPC Edition

    Reference: page 28, July 2013 Product Use Rights.

73. **What are the down-edition rights for Windows Server 2012 Datacenter?**

    Any earlier version of Windows Server in the following editions can be deployed:

    - Standard
    - Enterprise
    - Web Server
    - HPC Edition

    Reference: page 27, July 2013 Product Use Rights.

Windows Server 2012

License Mobility

74. **Do any of the Windows Server 2012 licenses have License Mobility?**

    None of the Windows Server 2012 licenses have License Mobility through Software Assurance rights. A Windows Server 2012 External Connector license with active SA has License Mobility within Server Farms rights.

    Reference: page 25, July 2013 Product Use Rights.

Step-Up Licenses

75. **Can a Windows Server 2012 Standard license be stepped up to a Windows Server 2012 Datacenter license?**

    Yes, with active SA.

    Reference: pages 83–84, October 2013 Product List.

New Version Rights

76. **What are the new version rights for a Windows Server 2012 Standard license with SA?**

    For every license with active SA when Windows Server 2012 R2 first became available in October 2013, or later:

    - One Windows Server 2012 R2 Standard license

    Reference: page 182, November 2013 Product List.

77. **What are the new version rights for a Windows Server 2012 Datacenter license with SA?**

    For every license with active SA when Windows Server 2012 R2 first became available in October 2013, or later:

    - One Windows Server 2012 R2 Datacenter license

    Reference: page 182, November 2013 Product List.

Windows Server 2012

Prior Versions

78. **What is the prior version of Windows Server 2012 Standard?**
    Windows Server 2008 R2 Standard.

    Reference: page 184, October 2013 Product List.

79. **What is the prior version of Windows Server 2012 Datacenter?**
    Windows Server 2008 R2 Datacenter.

    Reference: page 183, October 2013 Product List.

80. **What is the prior version of the Windows Server 2012 External Connector license?**
    Windows Server 2008 External Connector license.

    Reference: page 25, August 2012 Product List.

Mainstream and Extended Support Dates

81. **When does mainstream support end for Windows Server 2012 Standard and Datacenter editions?**
    January 9, 2018.

    Reference: https://support.microsoft.com/en-us/lifecycle?p1=16526

82. **When does extended support end for Windows Server 2012 Standard and Datacenter editions?**
    January 10, 2023.

    Reference: https://support.microsoft.com/en-us/lifecycle?p1=16526

Retired Editions

83. **Which editions of Windows Server 2012 were retired when the 2012 R2 version was introduced?**
    None.

    Reference: page 25, November 2013 Product List.

Windows Server 2008 R2

Date Available

84. When was Windows Server 2008 R2 first available?

August 2009, with the exception of HPC Edition which was first available in September 2010.

Reference: page 25, August 2012 Product List.

Licenses

85. What are the different licenses available for Windows Server 2008 R2?
- Windows Server 2008 R2 Standard license
- Windows Server 2008 R2 Enterprise license
- Windows Server 2008 R2 Datacenter license
- Windows Server 2008 R2 HPC Edition license
- Windows Server 2008 R2 for Itanium Based Systems license
- Windows Web Server 2008 R2 license
- Windows Server 2008 CAL
- Windows Server 2008 External Connector license

Reference: page 25, August 2012 Product List.

Licensing Models

86. How is Windows Server 2008 R2 Standard licensed?

With the Server/CAL model.

Reference: pages 27–28, April 2012 Product Use Rights.

87. How is Windows Server 2008 R2 Enterprise licensed?

With the Server/CAL model.

Reference: pages 27–28, April 2012 Product Use Rights.

Windows Server 2008 R2

88. **How is Windows Server 2008 R2 Datacenter licensed?**
    With the Processor/CAL model.
    Reference: pages 27–28, April 2012 Product Use Rights.

89. **What is the minimum number of processors required for a server licensed with Windows Server 2008 R2 Datacenter edition?**
    Two.
    Reference: page 27, April 2012 Product Use Rights.

90. **How is Windows Server 2008 R2 HPC Edition licensed?**
    With the Server licensing model.
    Reference: page 71, April 2012 Product Use Rights.

91. **How is Windows Server 2008 R2 for Itanium Based Systems licensed?**
    With the Processor/CAL model.
    Reference: pages 27–28, April 2012 Product Use Rights.

92. **What is the minimum number of processors required for a server licensed with Windows Server 2008 R2 for Itanium Based Systems edition?**
    Two.
    Reference: page 27, April 2012 Product Use Rights.

93. **How is Windows Web Server 2008 R2 licensed?**
    With the Server licensing model.
    Reference: page 71, April 2012 Product Use Rights.

Windows Server 2008 R2

CALs

94. **Which licenses can be used to access the editions of Windows Server 2008 R2 licensed with CALs?**
    - Windows Server 2008 CAL

    Alternatively, any of the following licenses can be used as long as they had active SA on February 1, 2008, or they were purchased after this date:
    - BackOffice CAL
    - Core CAL Suite
    - Enterprise CAL Suite

    As a final alternative, any of the following licenses can be used as long as they had active SA on March 1, 2011, or they were purchased after this date:
    - Core CAL Suite Bridge for Office 365
    - Core CAL Suite Bridge for Intune
    - Core CAL Suite Bridge for Office 365 and Intune
    - Enterprise CAL Suite Bridge for Office 365
    - Enterprise CAL Suite Bridge for Intune
    - Enterprise CAL Suite Bridge for Office 365 and Intune

    Reference: pages 30, 32, 33 & 35, April 2012 Product Use Rights.

95. **Are Windows Server 2008 CALs used to access Windows Server 2008 R2?**
    Yes.
    Reference: pages 30, 32, 33 & 35, April 2012 Product Use Rights.

96. **Are there Windows Server 2008 R2 CALs?**
    No, the Windows Server 2008 CALs were not updated when the Windows Server 2008 R2 licenses were released.
    Reference: page 25, August 2012 Product List.

Windows Server 2008 R2

97. **Can Windows Server 2008 CALs be used to access all editions of Windows Server 2008 R2 requiring CALs?**
Yes.

Reference: pages 30, 32, 33 & 35, April 2012 Product Use Rights.

98. **Are Windows Server 2008 CALs available as both Device and User CALs?**
Yes.

Reference: page 25, August 2012 Product List.

99. **Are CALs required to access a Windows Server 2008 R2 physical environment that is used solely to host and manage virtual machines?**
No.

Reference: pages 27–28, April 2012 Product Use Rights.

Per Server Mode

100. **Can Windows Server 2008 R2 Standard be licensed in Per Server mode?**
Yes.

Reference: pages 33–34, April 2012 Product Use Rights.

101. **Can Windows Server 2008 R2 Enterprise be licensed in Per Server mode?**
Yes.

Reference: pages 32–33, April 2012 Product Use Rights.

102. **Can Windows Server 2008 R2 Datacenter be licensed in Per Server mode?**
Yes.

Reference: pages 30–31, April 2012 Product Use Rights.

Windows Server 2008 R2

103. **Can Windows Server 2008 R2 for Itanium Based Systems be licensed in Per Server mode?**
Yes.
Reference: pages 35–36, April 2012 Product Use Rights.

External Users

104. **How are external users licensed for Windows Server 2008 R2 Standard?**
    - Windows Server 2008 CAL, or
    - Windows Server 2008 External Connector license

    Reference: pages 27–28, April 2012 Product Use Rights.

105. **How are external users licensed for Windows Server 2008 R2 Enterprise?**
    - Windows Server 2008 CAL, or
    - Windows Server 2008 External Connector license

    Reference: pages 27–28, April 2012 Product Use Rights.

106. **How are external users licensed for Windows Server 2008 R2 Datacenter?**
    - Windows Server 2008 CAL, or
    - Windows Server 2008 External Connector license

    Reference: pages 27–28, April 2012 Product Use Rights.

107. **How are external users licensed for Windows Server 2008 R2 HPC Edition?**
    They are covered by the Server license.
    Reference: page 71, April 2012 Product Use Rights.

108. **How are external users licensed for Windows Server 2008 R2 for Itanium Based Systems?**
    - Windows Server 2008 CAL, or
    - Windows Server 2008 External Connector license

    Reference: pages 27–28, April 2012 Product Use Rights.

109. How are external users licensed for Windows Web Server 2008 R2?

They are covered by the Server license.

Reference: page 71, April 2012 Product Use Rights.

110. How is the Windows Server 2008 External Connector license used?

One Windows Server 2008 External Connector license must be assigned to each physical server accessed by external users. The server itself must be licensed in the usual way for Windows Server 2008 R2 using Standard, Enterprise, Datacenter or Itanium Based Systems licenses.

Reference: page 28, April 2012 Product Use Rights.

111. Is there a Windows Server 2008 R2 External Connector license?

No, the Windows Server 2008 External Connector license was not updated when the Windows Server 2008 R2 licenses were released.

Reference: page 25, August 2012 Product List.

Virtualization Licensing

112. How is Windows Server 2008 R2 Standard licensed in a virtualized environment?

A Server license is assigned to the physical server and allows the running of Windows Server in a single virtual machine. Additional licenses can be assigned to the server to allow another virtual machine to be run per license. Windows Server can also be installed on the physical server but in this case may only be used to manage the virtual machine.

Reference: page 34, April 2012 Product Use Rights.

Windows Server 2008 R2

113. How is Windows Server 2008 R2 Enterprise licensed in a virtualized environment?

A Server license is assigned to the physical server and allows the running of Windows Server in up to four virtual machines. Additional licenses can be assigned to the server to allow four more virtual machines to be run per license. Windows Server can also be installed on the physical server, but in this case may only be used to manage the virtual machines.

Reference: page 33, April 2012 Product Use Rights.

114. How is Windows Server 2008 R2 Datacenter licensed in a virtualized environment?

All physical processors on the server must be licensed with Processor licenses and then unlimited virtual machines running Windows Server are permitted. Windows Server can also be installed on the physical server to run applications and/or to manage the virtual machines.

Reference: page 31, April 2012 Product Use Rights.

115. How is Windows Server 2008 R2 HPC Edition licensed in a virtualized environment?

A Server license is assigned to the physical server and allows the running of Windows Server in a single virtual machine. Additional licenses can be assigned to the server to allow another virtual machine to be run per license. Windows Server can also be installed on the physical server but in this case may only be used to manage the virtual machines.

Reference: pages 71 & 75, April 2012 Product Use Rights.

116. How is Windows Server 2008 R2 for Itanium Based Systems licensed in a virtualized environment?

All physical processors on the server must be licensed with Processor licenses and then unlimited virtual machines running Windows Server are permitted. Windows Server can also be installed on the physical server to run applications and/or to manage the virtual machines.

Reference: page 36, April 2012 Product Use Rights.

117. **How is Windows Web Server 2008 R2 licensed in a virtualized environment?**
A Server license is assigned to the physical server and allows the running of Windows Server in a single virtual machine. Additional licenses can be assigned to the server to allow another virtual machine to be run per license.

Reference: page 71, April 2012 Product Use Rights.

118. **Can different editions of Windows Server 2008 R2 be run in the virtual machines on a single physical server?**
Yes, as per the applicable downgrade/down-edition rights for the edition of Windows Server licensing the physical server.

Reference: pages 31 & 33, April 2012 Product Use Rights.

119. **How is the Windows Server 2008 External Connector license used in a virtualized environment?**
Each Windows Server 2008 External Connector license permits external users to access the physical server or any virtual machines running on that server.

Reference: page 28, April 2012 Product Use Rights.

Down-Edition Rights

120. **Are there down-edition rights for Windows Server 2008 R2 Standard?**
No.

Reference: page 34, April 2012 Product Use Rights.

121. **What are the down-edition rights for Windows Server 2008 R2 Enterprise?**
Any earlier version of Windows Server in the following edition can be deployed:
- Standard

Reference: page 33, April 2012 Product Use Rights.

Windows Server 2008 R2

122. What are the down-edition rights for Windows Server 2008 R2 Datacenter?

Any earlier version of Windows Server in the following editions can be deployed:
- Standard
- Enterprise

Reference: page 31, April 2012 Product Use Rights.

123. Are there down-edition rights for Windows Server 2008 R2 HPC Edition?

No.

Reference: page 75, April 2012 Product Use Rights.

124. Are there down-edition rights for Windows Server 2008 R2 for Itanium Based Systems?

No.

Reference: page 36, April 2012 Product Use Rights.

125. Are there down-edition rights for Windows Web Server 2008 R2?

No.

Reference: page 77, April 2012 Product Use Rights.

License Mobility

126. Do any of the Windows Server 2008 R2 licenses have License Mobility?

None of the Windows Server 2008 R2 licenses have License Mobility through Software Assurance rights. A Windows Server 2008 External Connector license has License Mobility within Server Farms rights.

Reference: page 28, April 2012 Product Use Rights.

Windows Server 2008 R2

Step-Up Licenses

127. Can a Windows Server 2008 R2 Standard license be stepped up to a Windows Server 2008 R2 Enterprise license?
Yes, with active SA.

Reference: pages 76–77, August 2012 Product List.

128. Can a Windows Server 2008 R2 Standard license be stepped up to a Windows Server 2008 R2 Datacenter license?
Yes, with active SA.

Reference: pages 76–77, August 2012 Product List.

129. Can a Windows Server 2008 R2 Enterprise license be stepped up to a Windows Server 2008 R2 Datacenter license?
Yes, with active SA.

Reference: pages 76–77, August 2012 Product List.

130. Can a license for Windows Server 2008 R2 HPC Edition, Itanium Based Systems or Web Server be stepped up to any other Windows Server 2008 R2 edition license?
No.

Reference: pages 76–77, August 2012 Product List.

New Version Rights

131. What are the New Version rights for a Windows Server 2008 R2 Standard license with SA?
For every license with active SA when Windows Server 2012 first became available in August 2012, or later:
- One Windows Server 2012 Standard license, or
- Two Windows Server 2012 Standard licenses if the original license was assigned to a server with more than two physical processors

Reference: page 166, September 2012 Product List.

Windows Server 2008 R2

132. **What are the new version rights for a Windows Server 2008 R2 Enterprise license with SA?**

    For every license with active SA when Windows Server 2012 first became available in August 2012, or later:
    - Two Windows Server 2012 Standard licenses, or
    - Three Windows Server 2012 Standard licenses if the original license was covered with active SA acquired or renewed between April 1, 2012 and August 31, 2012, or
    - Four Windows Server 2012 Standard licenses if the original license was assigned to a server with more than four physical processors

    Reference: page 164, September 2012 Product List.

133. **What are the new version rights for a Windows Server 2008 R2 Datacenter license with SA?**

    For every two licenses with active SA when Windows Server 2012 first became available in August 2012, or later:
    - One Windows Server 2012 Datacenter license

    Reference: pages 165–166, September 2012 Product List.

134. **What are the rules for upgrading an odd number of Windows Server 2008 R2 Datacenter licenses with active SA?**

    The total number of licenses is rounded down to the nearest even number and then divided by 2. For example, seven Windows Server 2008 R2 Datacenter licenses would be rounded down to six licenses, and then dividing by 2 gives rights to three Windows Server 2012 Datacenter licenses.

    Reference: pages 165–166, September 2012 Product List.

135. **What are the new version rights for a Windows Server 2008 R2 HPC Edition license with SA?**

    For every two licenses with active SA when Windows Server 2012 first became available in August 2012, or later:
    - One Windows Server 2012 Standard license

    Reference: pages 163–164, September 2012 Product List.

Windows Server 2008 R2

136. What are the rules for upgrading an odd number of Windows Server 2008 R2 HPC Edition licenses?

The total number of licenses is rounded up to the nearest even number and then divided by 2. For example, five Windows Server 2008 R2 HPC Edition licenses would be rounded up to six licenses, and then dividing by 2 gives rights to three Windows Server 2012 Standard licenses.

Reference: pages 163–164, September 2012 Product List.

137. What are the new version rights for a Windows Server 2008 R2 for Itanium Based Systems license with SA?

For every two licenses with active SA when Windows Server 2012 first became available in August 2012, or later:

- One Windows Server 2012 Datacenter license

Reference: pages 164–165, September 2012 Product List.

138. What are the rules for upgrading an odd number of Windows Server 2008 R2 for Itanium Based Systems licenses?

The total number of licenses is rounded down to the nearest even number and then divided by 2. For example, seven Windows Server 2008 R2 for Itanium Based Systems licenses would be rounded down to six licenses, and then dividing by 2 gives rights to three Windows Server 2012 Datacenter licenses.

Reference: pages 164–165, September 2012 Product List.

139. What are the new version rights for a Windows Web Server 2008 R2 license with SA?

For every two licenses with active SA when Windows Server 2012 first became available in August 2012, or later:

- One Windows Server 2012 Standard license

Reference: pages 166–167, September 2012 Product List.

Windows Server 2008 R2

140. What are the rules for upgrading an odd number of Windows Web Server 2008 R2 licenses?

The total number of licenses is rounded up to the nearest even number and then divided by 2. For example, five Windows Web Server 2008 R2 licenses would be rounded up to six licenses, and then dividing by 2 gives rights to three Windows Server 2012 Standard licenses.

Reference: pages 166–167, September 2012 Product List.

141. What are the new version rights for a Windows Server 2008 External Connector license with SA?

For every license with active SA when the Windows Server 2012 External Connector license was made available in August 2012, or later:

- One Windows Server 2012 External Connector license

Reference: page 25, September 2012 Product List.

Prior Versions

142. What is the prior version of Windows Server 2008 R2 Standard?

Windows Server 2008 Standard.

Reference: page 168, August 2012 Product List.

143. What is the prior version of Windows Server 2008 R2 Enterprise?

Windows Server 2008 Enterprise.

Reference: page 167, August 2012 Product List.

144. What is the prior version of Windows Server 2008 R2 Datacenter?

Windows Server 2008 Datacenter.

Reference: page 167, August 2012 Product List.

145. What is the prior version of Windows Server 2008 R2 HPC Edition?

Windows Server 2008 HPC Edition.

Reference: page 167, August 2012 Product List.

146. **What is the prior version of Windows Server 2008 R2 for Itanium Based Systems?**
Windows Server 2008 for Itanium Based Systems.

Reference: page 167, August 2012 Product List.

147. **What is the prior version of Windows Web Server 2008 R2?**
Windows Web Server 2008.

Reference: page 22, August 2009 Product List.

148. **What is the prior version of the Windows Server 2008 External Connector license?**
Windows Server 2003 External Connector license.

Reference: pages 20–21, February 2008 Product List.

Mainstream and Extended Support Dates

149. **When did mainstream support end for Windows Server 2008 R2?**
January 13, 2015, with the exception of Windows Web Server 2008 R2 which ended on July 9, 2013.

Reference: https://support.microsoft.com/en-us/lifecycle?p1=14134 and https://support.microsoft.com/en-us/lifecycle?C2=1163 (for Windows Server 2008 R2 HPC Edition).

150. **When does extended support end for Windows Server 2008 R2?**
January 14, 2020 with the exception of Windows Web Server 2008 R2 which ends on July 10, 2018.

Reference: https://support.microsoft.com/en-us/lifecycle?p1=14134 and https://support.microsoft.com/en-us/lifecycle?C2=1163 (for Windows Server 2008 R2 HPC Edition).

Windows Server 2008 R2

Retired Editions

151. Which editions of Windows Server 2008 R2 were retired when the 2012 version was introduced?
- Windows Server 2008 R2 Enterprise
- Windows Server 2008 R2 HPC Edition
- Windows Server 2008 R2 for Itanium Based Systems
- Windows Web Server 2008

Reference: pages 163–167, September 2012 Product List.

Windows Server 2008

Date Available

152. When was Windows Server 2008 first available?

March 2008, with the exception of:
- Windows Server 2008 High Performance Computing Edition which was first available in October 2008
- Windows Server 2008 High Performance Computing Edition without Hyper-V which was first available in November 2008

Reference: page 22, August 2009 Product List.

Licenses

153. What are the different licenses available for Windows Server 2008?
- Windows Server 2008 Standard license
- Windows Server 2008 Standard without Hyper-V license
- Windows Server 2008 Enterprise license
- Windows Server 2008 Enterprise without Hyper-V license
- Windows Server 2008 Datacenter license
- Windows Server 2008 Datacenter without Hyper-V license
- Windows Server 2008 High Performance Computing (HPC) Edition license
- Windows Server 2008 High Performance Computing (HPC) Edition without Hyper-V license
- Windows Server 2008 for Itanium Based Systems license
- Windows Web Server 2008 license
- Windows Server 2008 CAL
- Windows Server 2008 External Connector license

Reference: page 22, August 2009 Product List.

Windows Server 2008

Licensing Models

154. Are there any differences in the licensing between the regular editions and the "without Hyper-V" editions?
No.
Reference: page 27, January 2009 Product Use Rights.

155. How is Windows Server 2008 Standard licensed?
With the Server/CAL model.
Reference: pages 30–31, April 2009 Product Use Rights.

156. How is Windows Server 2008 Enterprise licensed?
With the Server/CAL model.
Reference: pages 30–31, April 2009 Product Use Rights.

157. How is Windows Server 2008 Datacenter licensed?
With the Processor/CAL model.
Reference: pages 30–31, April 2009 Product Use Rights.

158. What is the minimum number of processors required for a server licensed with Windows Server 2008 Datacenter?
Two.
Reference: page 40, April 2009 Product Use Rights.

159. How is Windows Server 2008 HPC Edition licensed?
With the Server licensing model.
Reference: pages 75–76, April 2009 Product Use Rights.

160. How is Windows Server 2008 for Itanium Based Systems licensed?
With the Processor/CAL model.
Reference: pages 30–31, April 2009 Product Use Rights.

161. How is Windows Web Server 2008 licensed?
With the Server licensing model.

Reference: pages 75–76, April 2009 Product Use Rights.

CALs

162. Which licenses can be used to access the editions of Windows Server 2008 licensed with CALs?
- Windows Server 2008 CAL

Alternatively, any of the following licenses can be used as long as they had active SA on February 1, 2008, or they were purchased after this date:
- BackOffice CAL
- Core CAL Suite
- Enterprise CAL Suite

Reference: page 34, April 2009 Product Use Rights.

163. Can Windows Server 2008 CALs be used to access all editions of Windows Server 2008 requiring CALs?
Yes.

Reference: page 34, April 2009 Product Use Rights.

164. Are Windows Server 2008 CALs available as both Device and User CALs?
Yes.

Reference: page 22, August 2009 Product List.

165. Are CALs required to access a Windows Server 2008 physical environment that is used solely to host and manage virtual machines?
No.

Reference: page 33, April 2009 Product Use Rights.

Windows Server 2008

166. **Is a CAL required for a user or device that accesses Windows Server 2008 only through the Internet without being authenticated?**
No.
Reference: page 33, April 2009 Product Use Rights.

Per Server Mode

167. **Can Windows Server 2008 Standard be licensed in Per Server mode?**
Yes.
Reference: page 41, April 2009 Product Use Rights.

168. **Can Windows Server 2008 Enterprise be licensed in Per Server mode?**
Yes.
Reference: page 41, April 2009 Product Use Rights.

External Users

169. **How are external users licensed for Windows Server 2008 Standard?**
- Windows Server 2008 CAL, or
- Windows Server 2008 External Connector license

Reference: pages 30 & 35, April 2009 Product Use Rights.

170. **How are external users licensed for Windows Server 2008 Enterprise?**
- Windows Server 2008 CAL, or
- Windows Server 2008 External Connector license

Reference: pages 30 & 35, April 2009 Product Use Rights.

Windows Server 2008

171. How are external users licensed for Windows Server 2008 Datacenter?
- Windows Server 2008 CAL, or
- Windows Server 2008 External Connector license

Reference: pages 30 & 35, April 2009 Product Use Rights.

172. How are external users licensed for Windows Server 2008 HPC Edition?
They are covered by the Server license.

Reference: page 76, April 2009 Product Use Rights.

173. How are external users licensed for Windows Server 2008 for Itanium Based Systems?
- Windows Server 2008 CAL, or
- Windows Server 2008 External Connector license

Reference: pages 30 & 35, April 2009 Product Use Rights.

174. How are external users licensed for Windows Web Server 2008?
They are covered by the Server license.

Reference: page 76, April 2009 Product Use Rights.

175. How is the Windows Server 2008 External Connector license used?
One Windows Server 2008 External Connector license must be assigned to each physical server accessed by external users. The server itself must be licensed in the usual way for Windows Server 2008 using Standard, Enterprise, Datacenter or Itanium Based Systems licenses.

Reference: page 35, April 2009 Product Use Rights.

Windows Server 2008

Virtualization Licensing

176. How is Windows Server 2008 Standard licensed in a virtualized environment?

A Server license is assigned to the physical server and allows the running of Windows Server in a single virtual machine. Additional licenses can be assigned to the server to allow another virtual machine to be run per license. Windows Server can also be installed on the physical server but in this case may only be used to manage the virtual machines.

Reference: page 40, April 2009 Product Use Rights.

177. How is Windows Server 2008 Enterprise licensed in a virtualized environment?

A Server license is assigned to the physical server and allows the running of Windows Server in up to four virtual machines. Additional licenses can be assigned to the server to allow four more virtual machines to be run per license. Windows Server can also be installed on the physical server but in this case may only be used to manage the virtual machines.

Reference: pages 40–41, April 2009 Product Use Rights.

178. How is Windows Server 2008 Datacenter licensed in a virtualized environment?

All physical processors on the server must be licensed with Processor licenses, where one license covers one processor, and then unlimited virtual machines running Windows Server are allowed. Windows Server can also be installed on the physical server to run applications and/or to manage the virtual machines.

Reference: pages 30–31, April 2009 Product Use Rights.

Windows Server 2008

179. How is Windows Server 2008 HPC Edition licensed in a virtualized environment?

A Server license is assigned to the physical server and allows the running of Windows Server in a single virtual machine. Additional licenses can be assigned to the server to allow another virtual machine to be run per license. Windows Server can also be installed on the physical server, but in this case may only be used to manage the virtual machines.

Reference: pages 75 & 77, April 2009 Product Use Rights.

180. How is Windows Server 2008 for Itanium Based Systems licensed in a virtualized environment?

All physical processors on the server must be licensed with Processor licenses, where one license covers one processor, and then unlimited virtual machines running Windows Server are allowed. Windows Server can also be installed on the physical server to run applications and/or to manage the virtual machines.

Reference: pages 30–31, April 2009 Product Use Rights.

181. How is Windows Web Server 2008 licensed in a virtualized environment?

A Server license is assigned to the physical server and allows the running of Windows Server in a single virtual machine. Additional licenses can be assigned to the server to allow another virtual machine to be run per license.

Reference: page 75, April 2009 Product Use Rights.

182. Can different editions of Windows Server 2008 be run in the virtual machines on a single physical server?

Yes, as per the applicable downgrade/down-edition rights for the edition of Windows Server licensing the physical server.

Reference: pages 40–41, April 2009 Product Use Rights.

Windows Server 2008

183. How is the Windows Server 2008 External Connector license used in a virtualized environment?

Each Windows Server 2008 External Connector license permits external users to access the physical server or any virtual machines running on that server.

Reference: page 35, April 2009 Product Use Rights.

Down-Edition Rights

184. Are there down-edition rights for Windows Server 2008 Standard?

No.

Reference: page 40, April 2009 Product Use Rights.

185. What are the down-edition rights for Windows Server 2008 Enterprise?

Any earlier version of Windows Server in the following edition can be deployed:

- Standard

Reference: pages 40–41, April 2009 Product Use Rights.

186. What are the down-edition rights for Windows Server 2008 Datacenter?

Any earlier version of Windows Server in the following editions can be deployed:

- Standard
- Enterprise

Reference: page 40, April 2009 Product Use Rights.

187. Are there down-edition rights for Windows Server 2008 HPC Edition?

No.

Reference: page 77, April 2009 Product Use Rights.

Windows Server 2008

188. Are there down-edition rights for Windows Server 2008 for Itanium Based Systems?
No.

Reference: pages 38–43, April 2009 Product Use Rights.

189. Are there down-edition rights for Windows Web Server 2008?
No.

Reference: pages 75–80, April 2009 Product Use Rights.

License Mobility

190. Do any of the Windows Server 2008 licenses have License Mobility?
None of the Windows Server 2008 licenses have License Mobility through Software Assurance rights. A Windows Server 2008 External Connector license has License Mobility within Server Farms rights.

Reference: page 38, April 2009 Product Use Rights.

Step-Up Licenses

191. Can a Windows Server 2008 Standard license be stepped up to a Windows Server 2008 Enterprise license?
Yes, with active SA.

Reference: pages 75–77, August 2009 Product List.

192. Can a Windows Server 2008 Standard license be stepped up to a Windows Server 2008 Datacenter license?
Yes, with active SA.

Reference: pages 75–77, August 2009 Product List.

193. Can a Windows Server 2008 Enterprise license be stepped up to a Windows Server 2008 Datacenter license?
Yes, with active SA.

Reference: pages 75–77, August 2009 Product List.

Windows Server 2008

194. Can a license for Windows Server 2008 HPC Edition, Itanium Based Systems or Web Server be stepped up to any other Windows Server 2008 edition license?
No.

Reference: pages 75–77, August 2009 Product List.

195. Can a license for the "without Hyper-V" editions be stepped up to a license for any of the regular editions?
No.

Reference: pages 75–77, August 2009 Product List.

New Version Rights

196. What are the new version rights for a Windows Server 2008 Standard license with SA?
For every license with active SA on September 1, 2009, or later:
- One Windows Server 2008 R2 Standard license

Reference: page 132, September 2009 Product List.

197. What are the new version rights for a Windows Server 2008 Enterprise license with SA?
For every license with active SA on September 1, 2009, or later:
- One Windows Server 2008 R2 Enterprise license

Reference: page 132, September 2009 Product List.

198. What are the new version rights for a Windows Server 2008 Datacenter license with SA?
For every license with active SA on September 1, 2009, or later:
- One Windows Server 2008 R2 Datacenter license

Reference: page 131, September 2009 Product List.

199. What are the new version rights for a Windows Server 2008 HPC Edition license with SA?

For every license with active SA when Windows Server 2008 R2 HPC Edition was made available in September 2010:

- One Windows Server 2008 R2 HPC Edition license

Reference: page 136, September 2010 Product List.

200. What are the new version rights for a Windows Server 2008 for Itanium Based Systems license with SA?

For every license with active SA on September 1, 2009, or later:

- One Windows Server 2008 R2 for Itanium Based Systems license

Reference: page 132, September 2009 Product List.

201. What are the new version rights for a Windows Web Server 2008 license with SA?

For every license with active SA when Windows Web Server 2008 R2 was made available in August 2009, or later:

- One Windows Web Server 2008 R2 license

Reference: page 22, September 2009 Product List.

202. What are the new version rights for a Windows Server 2008 External Connector license with SA?

For every license with active SA when the Windows Server 2012 External Connector license was made available in August 2012, or later:

- One Windows Server 2012 External Connector license

Reference: page 25, September 2012 Product List.

Windows Server 2008

Prior Versions

203. What is the prior version of Windows Server 2008 Standard?
Windows Server 2003 R2 Standard.

Reference: page 131, August 2009 Product List.

204. What is the prior version of Windows Server 2008 Enterprise?
Windows Server 2003 R2 Enterprise.

Reference: page 131, August 2009 Product List.

205. What is the prior version of Windows Server 2008 Datacenter?
Windows Server 2003 R2 Datacenter.

Reference: pages 130–131, August 2009 Product List.

206. What is the prior version of Windows Server 2008 HPC Edition?
Windows Server Compute Cluster Edition 2003.

Reference: page 131, August 2009 Product List.

207. What is the prior version of Windows Server 2008 for Itanium Based Systems?
This was a new edition, so had no prior version.

Reference: pages 20–21, February 2008 Product List.

208. What is the prior version of Windows Web Server 2008?
Windows Server 2003 Web Edition.

Reference: pages 20–21, February 2008 Product List.

209. What is the prior version of the Windows Server 2008 External Connector license?
Windows Server 2003 External Connector license.

Reference: pages 20–21, February 2008 Product List.

Windows Server 2008

Mainstream and Extended Support Dates

210. When did mainstream support end for Windows Server 2008?
January 13, 2015, with the exception of Windows Web Server 2008 which ended on July 9, 2013.

Reference: https://support.microsoft.com/en-us/lifecycle?p1=12925 and https://support.microsoft.com/en-us/lifecycle?p1=13582 (Windows Server 2008 HPC Edition).

211. When does extended support end for Windows Server 2008?
January 14, 2020 with the exception of Windows Web Server 2008 which ends on July 10, 2018.

Reference: https://support.microsoft.com/en-us/lifecycle?p1=12925 and https://support.microsoft.com/en-us/lifecycle?p1=13582 (Windows Server 2008 HPC Edition).

Retired Editions

212. Which editions of Windows Server 2008 were retired when the 2008 R2 version was introduced?
None.

Reference: page 22, September 2009 Product List.

… *Windows Server 2003 R2*

Windows Server 2003 R2

Licenses

213. **What are the different licenses available for Windows Server 2003 R2?**
     - Windows Server 2003 R2 Standard Edition license
     - Windows Server 2003 R2 Enterprise Edition license
     - Windows Server 2003 R2 Datacenter Edition license
     - Windows Server 2003 Web Edition license
     - Windows Server Compute Cluster Edition 2003 license
     - Windows Server 2003 CAL
     - Windows Server 2003 External Connector license

     Reference: pages 20–21, February 2008 Product List.

Mainstream and Extended Support Dates

214. **What are the key dates for Windows Server 2003 R2 Standard?**
     - Mainstream support end date – July 13, 2010
     - Extended support end date – July 14, 2015

     Reference: https://support.microsoft.com/en-us/lifecycle?p1=10394

215. **What are the key dates for Windows Server 2003 R2 Enterprise?**
     - Mainstream support end date – July 13, 2010
     - Extended support end date – July 14, 2015

     Reference: https://support.microsoft.com/en-us/lifecycle?p1=10394

216. **What are the key dates for Windows Server 2003 R2 Datacenter?**
     - Mainstream support end date – July 13, 2010
     - Extended support end date – July 14, 2015

     Reference: https://support.microsoft.com/en-us/lifecycle?p1=10394

217. What are the key dates for Windows Server 2003 Web Edition?
- Mainstream support end date – July 13, 2010
- Extended support end date – July 14, 2015

Reference: https://support.microsoft.com/en-us/lifecycle?p1=3198

218. What are the key dates for Windows Server Compute Cluster Edition 2003?
- Mainstream support end date – July 13, 2010
- Extended support end date – July 14, 2015

Reference: https://support.microsoft.com/en-us/lifecycle?C2=11765

Windows Server 2003

Licenses

219. **What are the different licenses available for Windows Server 2003?**
     - Windows Server 2003 Standard Edition license
     - Windows Server 2003 Enterprise Edition license
     - Windows Server 2003 Web Edition license
     - Windows Server 2003 CAL
     - Windows Server 2003 External Connector license

     Reference: page 21, January 2006 Product List.

Mainstream and Extended Support Dates

220. **What are the key dates for Windows Server 2003 Standard?**
     - Mainstream support end date – July 13, 2010
     - Extended support end date – July 14, 2015

     Reference: https://support.microsoft.com/en-us/lifecycle?p1=3198

221. **What are the key dates for Windows Server 2003 Enterprise?**
     - Mainstream support end date – July 13, 2010
     - Extended support end date – July 14, 2015

     Reference: https://support.microsoft.com/en-us/lifecycle?p1=3198

222. **What are the key dates for Windows Server 2003 Web Edition?**
     - Mainstream support end date – July 13, 2010
     - Extended support end date – July 14, 2015

     Reference: https://support.microsoft.com/en-us/lifecycle?p1=3198

Datacenter Edition

223. **Was Windows Server 2003 Datacenter Edition available through a Volume Licensing agreement?**
     No.

     Reference: page 21, January 2006 Product List.

Windows Server 2000

Licenses

224. What are the different licenses available for Windows Server 2000?
- Windows 2000 Server license
- Windows 2000 Advanced Server license
- Windows Server 2000 CAL
- Windows Server 2000 Internet Connector license

Reference: page 3, January 2003 Product List.

Mainstream and Extended Support Dates

225. What are the key dates for Windows Server 2000?
- Mainstream support end date – June 30, 2005
- Extended support end date – July 13, 2010

Reference: https://support.microsoft.com/en-us/lifecycle?p1=7274

226. What are the key dates for Windows Server 2000 Advanced Server?
- Mainstream support end date – June 30, 2005
- Extended support end date – July 13, 2010

Reference: https://support.microsoft.com/en-us/lifecycle?p1=7017

Datacenter Server

227. Was Windows 2000 Datacenter Server available through a Volume Licensing agreement?
No.

Reference: page 3, January 2003 Product List.

Licensing Windows Server in Microsoft Azure

Azure Windows Server Virtual Machines

228. **Can an organization buy an Azure virtual machine which includes Windows Server?**

    Yes, the cost of a Windows Server virtual machine in Azure includes the cost of the Windows Server license.

    Reference: https://azure.microsoft.com/en-us/pricing/licensing-faq

229. **Are Windows Server CALs required for users or devices accessing an Azure virtual machine which includes Windows Server?**

    No.

    Reference: https://azure.microsoft.com/en-us/pricing/licensing-faq

230. **Can an organization pay for an Azure virtual machine which includes Windows Server through a Volume Licensing agreement?**

    Yes, it's a compute service which can be paid for through the Open agreements, MPSA, or Enterprise Agreements including the Server and Cloud Enrollment.

    Reference: https://azure.microsoft.com/en-us/pricing

Using Windows Server Standard Licenses

231. **Can a Windows Server Standard license acquired through a Volume Licensing agreement be used to license an Azure virtual machine?**

    Yes, the Azure Hybrid Use Benefit allows a Windows Server Standard license with SA to be assigned to an Azure virtual machine to license it for Windows Server.

    Reference: pages 49–50, March 2016 Product Terms.

232. How many Azure virtual machines does a Windows Server Standard license with SA cover under the Hybrid Use Benefit?
Either two virtual machines with 1 to 8 cores each, or one virtual machine with up to 16 cores.

Reference: pages 49–50, March 2016 Product Terms.

233. If a Windows Server Standard license with SA has been assigned to an Azure virtual machine, can it be reassigned back to an on-premises server under the Hybrid Use Benefit?
Yes, but no more frequently than every 90 days.

Reference: pages 49–50, March 2016 Product Terms.

234. Can a Windows Server Standard license with SA be assigned to an Azure virtual machine AND an on-premises server under the Hybrid Use Benefit?
No, the Hybrid Use Benefit gives "alternative" rights for Windows Server Standard licenses; this means that an organization can opt to use the licenses for an Azure virtual machine or an on-premises server, but not both.

Reference: pages 49–50, March 2016 Product Terms.

Using Windows Server Datacenter Licenses

235. Can a Windows Server Datacenter license acquired through a Volume Licensing agreement be used to license an Azure virtual machine?
Yes, the Azure Hybrid Use Benefit allows a Windows Server Datacenter license with SA to be assigned to an Azure virtual machine to license it for Windows Server.

Reference: pages 49–50, March 2016 Product Terms.

Licensing Windows Server in Microsoft Azure

236. **How many Azure virtual machines does a Windows Server Datacenter license with SA cover under the Hybrid Use Benefit?**
Either two virtual machines with 1 to 8 cores each, or one virtual machine with up to 16 cores.

Reference: pages 49–50, March 2016 Product Terms.

237. **If a Windows Server Datacenter license with SA has been assigned to an Azure virtual machine, can it be reassigned back to an on-premises server?**
It doesn't need to be reassigned. The Hybrid Use Benefit gives "additive" rights for Windows Server Datacenter licenses; this means that the licenses may remain assigned to servers in an on-premises environment AND be used to license an Azure virtual machine.

Reference: pages 49–50, March 2016 Product Terms.

238. **Can a Windows Server Datacenter license with SA be assigned to an Azure virtual machine AND an on-premises server?**
Yes, the Hybrid Use Benefit gives "additive" rights for Windows Server Datacenter licenses; this means that the licenses may remain assigned to servers in an on-premises environment AND be used to license an Azure virtual machine.

Reference: pages 49–50, March 2016 Product Terms.

REMOTE DESKTOP SERVICES
General Licensing Questions

Availability

239. Is Windows Server Remote Desktop Services (RDS) available as a standalone server product?

No, it is only available as a component of Windows Server 2008 R2 and later.

Reference: page 44, March 2016 Product Terms.

240. Is Windows Server Terminal Services available as a standalone server product?

No, it is only available as a component of Windows Server 2008 and earlier.

Reference: page 22, August 2009 Product List.

Terminal Services

241. When did Terminal Services become Remote Desktop Services?

Terminal Services functionality was renamed Remote Desktop Services with the release of Windows Server 2008 R2.

Reference: page 5, July 2009 Product Use Rights.

CALs

242. Do RDS/Terminal Services CALs allow access to Remote Desktop Services/Terminal Services in earlier versions of Windows Server software?

Yes. For example, an RDS 2012 CAL allows access to Terminal Services on a server licensed with Windows Server 2008 Standard.

Reference: page 70, March 2016 Product Terms.

Remote Desktop Services: General Licensing Questions

243. Can RDS CALs be used to allow concurrent usage, rather than being assigned to specific users or devices?

No, this is known as Per Server mode and may only be used with Base CALs. RDS CALs are classified as Additive CALs and thus may not be used in Per Server mode.

Reference: pages 9 & 45, March 2016 Product Terms.

244. Can an RDS CAL be used to access a Windows Server running on a Service Provider's shared hardware?

Yes, as long as it is an RDS User CAL with active Software Assurance.

Reference: page 46, March 2016 Product Terms.

245. Can an RDS CAL be used to access a Windows Server Azure virtual machine?

Yes, as long as it is an RDS User CAL with active Software Assurance.

Reference: page 46, March 2016 Product Terms.

246. Can an RDS CAL be used to access a Windows Server virtual machine running on a Service Provider's shared hardware AND an on-premises server?

Yes, as long as it is an RDS User CAL with active Software Assurance.

Reference: https://azure.microsoft.com/en-us/pricing/licensing-faq

247. Can an RDS CAL be used to access a Windows Server Azure virtual machine AND an on-premises server?

Yes, as long as it is an RDS User CAL with active Software Assurance.

Reference: https://azure.microsoft.com/en-us/pricing/licensing-faq

Remote Desktop Services: General Licensing Questions

248. Can an RDS CAL be used to access a Windows Server virtual machine running on a Service Provider's shared hardware AND a Windows Server Azure virtual machine?
No.

Reference: https://azure.microsoft.com/en-us/pricing/licensing-faq

249. Can RDS Device CALs be switched to User CALs and vice versa?
Yes, but only when Software Assurance is renewed.

Reference: page 74, March 2016 Product Terms.

250. Do the Core or Enterprise CAL Suites include an RDS CAL?
No.

Reference: page 72, March 2016 Product Terms.

251. Are the access rights to Remote Desktop Services included in the VDI Suite the same as an RDS CAL?
No, an RDS CAL allows a licensed user or device to access a VDI desktop running on Windows Server OR a Windows Server session-based desktop. The VDI Suite only licenses the use of Remote Desktop Services for accessing a VDI desktop.

Reference: page 63, April 2015 Product Use Rights.

252. Are RDS CALs required to access a Microsoft Azure RemoteApp collection?
No.

Reference: https://azure.microsoft.com/en-in/documentation/articles/remoteapp-licensing

External Connector License

253. Does a Windows Server RDS/Terminal Services External Connector license allow access to Remote Desktop Services/Terminal Services in earlier versions of Windows Server software?

Yes. For example, a Windows Server 2008 Terminal Services External Connector license allows access to Terminal Services on a server licensed with Windows Server 2003 R2 Standard.

Reference: page 70, March 2016 Product Terms.

254. Is there a limit to the number of external users that can access a server licensed with an RDS/Terminal Services External Connector license?

No.

Reference: page 70, March 2016 Product Terms.

Application Virtualization for Remote Desktop Services

255. When was access to Microsoft Application Virtualization for Remote Desktop Services functionality first licensed with RDS licenses?

In January 2010, with the launch of Application Virtualization 4.6 for Remote Desktop Services, when the following licenses allowed access to this functionality:

- Windows Server 2008 Terminal Services CAL
- Windows Server 2008 RDS CAL
- Windows Server 2008 Terminal Services External Connector license
- Windows Server 2008 RDS External Connector license

Reference: pages 5, 36 & 38, January 2010 Product Use Rights.

Anonymous Use

256. What is anonymous use of RDS?

It's a right available as part of an MSDN subscription which allows up to 200 anonymous users at a time to use RDS to access an online demonstration of a customer's programs.

Reference: page 11, March 2016 Product Terms.

Windows Server 2012 RDS

Date Available

257. When was Windows Server 2012 RDS first available?
Windows Server 2012 RDS is a service of Windows Server 2012 which was first available in August 2012.

Reference: pages 25–26, October 2013 Product List.

Licenses

258. What are the different licenses available for Windows Server 2012 RDS?
- Windows Server 2012 RDS CAL
- Windows Server 2012 RDS USL
- Windows Server 2012 RDS External Connector license

Reference: pages 44 & 45, March 2016 Product Terms.

Licensing Model

259. How is Windows Server 2012 RDS licensed?
Windows Server RDS is a service of Windows Server 2012 and 2012 R2, so users or devices accessing Remote Desktop Services must first be licensed for access to the underlying Windows Server. Additionally, each user or device requires a Windows Server 2012 RDS CAL, or users may alternatively be licensed with a Windows Server 2012 RDS USL.

Reference: page 45, March 2016 Product Terms.

CALs

260. Can Windows Server 2012 RDS CALs be used to access Remote Desktop Services in Windows Server 2012 R2?
Yes.

Reference: page 45, March 2016 Product Terms.

261. Are there Windows Server 2012 R2 RDS CALs?

No, the Windows Server 2012 RDS CALs were not updated when the Windows Server 2012 R2 licenses were released.

Reference: page 44, March 2016 Product Terms.

262. Can Windows Server 2012 RDS CALs be used to access Remote Desktop Services in both Standard and Datacenter editions of Windows Server 2012 and 2012 R2?

Yes.

Reference: page 45, March 2016 Product Terms.

263. Are Windows Server 2012 RDS CALs available as both Device and User CALs?

Yes.

Reference: page 44, March 2016 Product Terms.

USL

264. When was the Windows Server 2012 RDS USL introduced?

This license first appeared in the July 2015 Product Terms document.

Reference: page 45, July 2015 Product Terms.

265. Through which Volume Licensing agreements can the Windows Server 2012 RDS USL be purchased?

Only the Enterprise Agreement and Enterprise Subscription Agreement.

Reference: refer to current Microsoft Price Lists.

External Users

266. How are external users licensed for Windows Server 2012 RDS?

In addition to being licensed for Windows Server 2012, one of the following licenses is required:
- Windows Server 2012 RDS CAL, or
- Windows Server 2012 RDS USL, or
- Windows Server 2012 RDS External Connector license

Reference: page 45, March 2016 Product Terms.

267. How is the Windows Server 2012 RDS External Connector license used?

One Windows Server 2012 RDS External Connector license must be assigned to each physical server accessed by external users. The server itself must be licensed in the usual way for Windows Server 2012 using either Standard or Datacenter edition licenses. In addition, a Windows Server 2012 External Connector license must also be assigned to the server.

Reference: pages 45 & 70, March 2016 Product Terms.

268. Is there a Windows Server 2012 R2 RDS External Connector license?

No, the Windows Server 2012 RDS External Connector license was not updated when the Windows Server 2012 R2 licenses were released.

Reference: page 44, March 2016 Product Terms.

License Mobility

269. Do any of the Windows Server 2012 RDS licenses have License Mobility?

A Windows Server 2012 RDS External Connector license with active SA has License Mobility across Server Farms rights.

Reference: page 24, Volume Licensing Brief: "Licensing Microsoft server products for use in virtual environments" – April 2014.

Prior Version

270. What is the prior version of the Windows Server 2012 RDS External Connector license?

Windows Server 2008 RDS External Connector license.

Reference: page 44, March 2016 Product Terms.

Windows Server 2008 RDS

Date Available

271. When was Windows Server 2008 RDS first available?

Windows Server 2008 RDS is a service of Windows Server 2008 R2 which was first available in August 2009.

Reference: page 25, August 2012 Product List.

Licenses

272. What are the different licenses available for Windows Server 2008 RDS?

- Windows Server 2008 RDS CAL
- Windows Server 2008 RDS External Connector license

Reference: page 25, August 2012 Product List.

Licensing Model

273. How is Windows Server 2008 RDS licensed?

Windows Server RDS is a service of Windows Server 2008 R2, so users or devices accessing the RDS service must first be licensed for access to the underlying Windows Server. Additionally, each user or device requires a Windows Server 2008 RDS CAL.

Reference: pages 30–31, 32, 33–34, & 35 April 2012 Product Use Rights.

CALs

274. Are there Windows Server 2008 R2 RDS CALs?

No, the Windows Server 2008 RDS CALs were released with Windows Server 2008 R2.

Reference: page 25, August 2012 Product List.

Windows Server 2008 RDS

275. Can Windows Server 2008 RDS CALs be used to access Remote Desktop Services in any edition of Windows Server 2008 R2 licensed with CALs?
Yes.

Reference: pages 30–31, 32, 33–34, & 35 April 2012 Product Use Rights.

276. Are Windows Server 2008 RDS CALs available as both Device and User CALs?
Yes.

Reference: page 28, April 2012 Product Use Rights.

277. Can Windows Server 2008 Terminal Services CALs be used to access Remote Desktop Services in Windows Server 2008 R2?
Yes.

Reference: pages 30–31, 32, 33–34, & 35 April 2012 Product Use Rights.

278. Are Windows Server 2008 RDS CALs and Windows Server 2008 Terminal Services CALs interchangeable?
Yes.

Reference: page 5, July 2009 Product Use Rights.

External Users

279. How are external users licensed for Windows Server 2008 RDS?
In addition to being licensed for Windows Server 2008 R2, one of the following licenses is required:
- Windows Server 2008 RDS CAL, or
- Windows Server 2008 RDS External Connector license

Reference: pages 27–28, April 2012 Product Use Rights.

Windows Server 2008 RDS

280. **Are external users licensed with Windows Server 2008 Terminal Services CALs or a Terminal Services External Connector license allowed to access Remote Desktop Services in Windows Server 2008 R2?**
Yes.

Reference: pages 30–31, 32, 33–34, & 35 April 2012 Product Use Rights.

281. **How is the Windows Server 2008 RDS External Connector license used?**
One Windows Server 2008 RDS External Connector license must be assigned to each physical server accessed by external users. The server itself must be licensed in the usual way for Windows Server 2008 using Standard, Enterprise, Datacenter or Itanium Based Systems licenses. In addition, a Windows Server 2008 External Connector license must also be assigned to the server.

Reference: pages 31, 32, 34 & 35 April 2012 Product Use Rights.

282. **Is there a Windows Server 2008 R2 RDS External Connector license?**
No, the Windows Server 2008 RDS External Connector license was released with Windows Server 2008 R2.

Reference: page 25, August 2012 Product List.

License Mobility

283. **Do any of the Windows Server 2008 RDS licenses have License Mobility?**
A Windows Server 2008 RDS External Connector license has License Mobility across Server Farm rights.

Reference: page 28, April 2012 Product Use Rights.

Windows Server 2008 RDS

New Version Rights

284. What are the new version rights for a Windows Server 2008 RDS External Connector license with SA?

For every license with active SA when Windows Server 2012 first became available in August 2012, or later:

- Windows Server 2012 RDS External Connector license

Reference: page 44, March 2016 Product Terms.

Prior Version

285. What is the prior version of the Windows Server 2008 RDS External Connector license?

Windows Server 2008 Terminal Services External Connector license.

Reference: page 22, August 2009 Product List.

Retired Licenses

286. Which Windows Server 2008 RDS licenses were retired when the 2012 version was introduced?

None.

Reference: page 44, March 2016 Product Terms.

Windows Server 2008 Terminal Services

Date Available

287. When was Windows Server 2008 Terminal Services first available?

Windows Server 2008 Terminal Services is a service of Windows Server 2008 which was first available in March 2008.

Reference: page 22, August 2009 Product List.

Licenses

288. What are the different licenses available for Windows Server 2008 Terminal Services?
- Windows Server 2008 Terminal Services CAL
- Windows Server 2008 Terminal Services External Connector license

Reference: page 22, August 2009 Product List.

Licensing Model

289. How is Windows Server 2008 Terminal Services licensed?

Terminal Services is a service of Windows Server 2008, so users or devices accessing Terminal Services must first be licensed for access to the underlying Windows Server. Additionally, each user or device requires a Windows Server 2008 Terminal Services CAL.

Reference: page 34, April 2009 Product Use Rights.

CALs

290. Are Windows Server 2008 Terminal Services CALs available as both Device and User CALs?
Yes.

Reference: page 35, April 2009 Product Use Rights.

External Users

291. How are external users licensed for Windows Server 2008 Terminal Services?

In addition to being licensed for Windows Server, one of the following licenses is required:
- Windows Server 2008 Terminal Services CAL, or
- Windows Server 2008 Terminal Services External Connector license

Reference: pages 34–36, April 2009 Product Use Rights.

292. How is the Windows Server 2008 Terminal Services External Connector license used?

One Windows Server 2008 Terminal Services External Connector license must be assigned to each physical server accessed by external users. The server itself must be licensed in the usual way for Windows Server 2008 using Standard, Enterprise, Datacenter or Itanium Based Systems licenses. In addition, a Windows Server 2008 External Connector license must also be assigned to the server.

Reference: pages 35 – 36, April 2009 Product Use Rights.

License Mobility

293. Do any of the Windows Server 2008 Terminal Services licenses have License Mobility?

A Windows Server 2008 Terminal Services External Connector license has License Mobility across Server Farm rights.

Reference: page 38, April 2009 Product Use Rights.

New Version Rights

294. What are the new version rights for a Windows Server 2008 Terminal Services External Connector license with SA?
For every license with active SA when Windows Server 2008 first became available in
- Windows Server 2008 RDS External Connector license

Reference: page 25, August 2012 Product List.

Prior Version

295. What is the prior version of the Windows Server 2008 Terminal Services External Connector license?
Windows Server 2003 Terminal Services External Connector license.

Reference: page 20, February 2008 Product List.

Retired Licenses

296. Which Windows Server 2008 Terminal Services licenses were retired when the 2008 RDS version was introduced?
None.

Reference: page 25, August 2012 Product List.

Windows Server 2003 Terminal Services

Licenses

297. What are the different licenses available for Windows Server 2003 Terminal Services?
- Windows Server 2003 Terminal Server CAL
- Windows Server 2003 Terminal Services External Connector license

Reference: page 21, January 2006 Product List.

Windows Server 2000 Terminal Services

Licenses

298. What are the different licenses available for Windows Server 2000 Terminal Services?
- Windows 2000 Terminal Server CAL
- Windows 2000 Terminal Services Internet Connector license

Reference: page 3, January 2003 Product List.

ACTIVE DIRECTORY RIGHTS MANAGEMENT SERVICES

General Licensing Questions

Availability

299. Is Windows Server Active Directory Rights Management Services (ADRMS) available as a standalone server product?

No, it is only available as a component of Windows Server.

Reference: page 44, March 2016 Product Terms.

300. What other names has Active Directory Rights Management Services been known as?

Windows Server 2003/2003 R2 – Rights Management Services 1.0

Reference: page 21, January 2006 Product List.

Windows Server 2008/2008 R2 – Rights Management Services.

Reference: page 22, August 2009 Product List.

Windows Server 2012/2012 R2 – Active Directory Rights Management Services.

Reference: page 25, October 2013 Product List.

CALs

301. Can RMS Device CALs be switched to User CALs and vice versa?

Yes, but only when Software Assurance is renewed.

Reference: page 74, March 2016 Product Terms.

302. Are RMS CALs available as both Device and User CALs?

Yes.

Reference: page 5, Volume Licensing Brief: "Base and Additive Client Access Licenses (CALs): An explanation" – August 2015.

303. Can RMS CALs be used to allow concurrent usage, rather than being assigned to specific users or devices?

No, this is known as Per Server mode and may only be used with Base CALs. RMS CALs are classified as Additive CALs and thus may not be used in Per Server mode.

Reference: pages 9 & 45, March 2016 Product Terms.

304. Do RMS CALs allow access to RMS in earlier versions of Windows Server software?

Yes. For example, a Windows Server 2012 ADRMS CAL allows access to RMS on a server licensed with Windows Server 2003 Standard.

Reference: page 70, March 2016 Product Terms.

External Connector License

305. Is there a limit to the number of external users that can access a server licensed with an RMS External Connector license?

No.

Reference: page 70, March 2016 Product Terms.

306. Does an RMS External Connector license allow access to RMS in earlier versions of Windows Server software?

Yes. For example, a Windows Server 2008 RMS External Connector license allows access to RMS on a server licensed with Windows Server 2003 R2 Standard.

Reference: page 70, March 2016 Product Terms.

Windows Server 2012 ADRMS

Date Available

307. When was Windows Server 2012 ADRMS first available?

Windows Server 2012 ADRMS is a service of Windows Server 2012 which was first available in August 2012.

Reference: page 25, October 2013 Product List.

Licenses

308. What are the different licenses available for Windows Server 2012 ADRMS?

- Windows Server 2012 ADRMS CAL
- Windows Server 2012 ADRMS External Connector license

Reference: page 44, March 2016 Product Terms.

Licensing Model

309. How is Windows Server 2012 ADRMS licensed?

Windows Server ADRMS is a service of Windows Server 2012 and 2012 R2, so users or devices accessing ADRMS must first be licensed for access to the underlying Windows Server. Additionally, each user or device requires a Windows Server 2012 ADRMS CAL.

Reference: page 45, March 2016 Product Terms.

Windows Server 2012 ADRMS

CALs

310. Which licenses, apart from ADRMS CALs, can be used to access Windows Server 2012 ADRMS?

- Enterprise Mobility Suite USL

Alternatively, the following license may be used if a user is also licensed for Windows Server 2012:

- Azure Rights Management USL

As a final alternative, any of the following licenses can be used as long as they had active SA in August 2012 when Windows Server 2012 was first made available, or they were purchased after that date:

- Enterprise CAL Suite
- Enterprise CAL Suite Bridge for Office 365
- Enterprise CAL Suite Bridge for Intune
- Enterprise CAL Suite Bridge for Office 365 and Intune

Reference: pages 45 & 72, March 2016 Product Terms.

311. Can Windows Server 2012 ADRMS CALs be used to access ADRMS in Windows Server 2012 R2?

Yes.

Reference: page 45, March 2016 Product Terms.

312. Are there Windows Server 2012 R2 ADRMS CALs?

No, the Windows Server 2012 ADRMS CALs were not updated when the Windows Server 2012 R2 licenses were released.

Reference: page 44, March 2016 Product Terms.

313. Can Windows Server 2012 ADRMS CALs be used to access ADRMS in both Standard and Datacenter editions of Windows Server 2012 and 2012 R2?

Yes.

Reference: page 45, March 2016 Product Terms.

314. Can Office 365 E3 and E4 USLs be used to access Windows Server 2012 ADRMS?

No, this right is no longer available. However, between July 2013 and April 2014 these licenses were listed as qualifying access licenses to ADRMS in the Products Use Rights document.

Reference: pages 25 & 27, April 2014 Product Use Rights.

USL

315. Is there a Windows Server 2012 ADRMS USL?

No.

Reference: page 45, March 2016 Product Terms.

External Users

316. How are external users licensed for Windows Server 2012 ADRMS?

In addition to being licensed for Windows Server 2012, one of the following licenses is required:
- Windows Server 2012 ADRMS CAL, or
- Windows Server 2012 ADRMS External Connector license

Reference: page 45, March 2016 Product Terms.

317. How is the Windows Server 2012 ADRMS External Connector license used?

One Windows Server 2012 ADRMS External Connector license must be assigned to each physical server accessed by external users. The server itself must be licensed in the usual way for Windows Server 2012 using either Standard or Datacenter edition licenses. In addition, a Windows Server 2012 External Connector license must also be assigned to the server.

Reference: pages 45 & 70, March 2016 Product Terms.

318. **Is there a Windows Server 2012 R2 ADRMS External Connector license?**
No, the Windows Server 2012 ADRMS External Connector license was not updated when the Windows Server 2012 R2 licenses were released.

Reference: page 44, March 2016 Product Terms.

License Mobility

319. **Do any of the Windows Server 2012 ADRMS licenses have License Mobility?**
A Windows Server 2012 ADRMS External Connector license with active SA has License Mobility across Server Farms rights.

Reference: page 24, Volume Licensing Brief: "Licensing Microsoft server products for use in virtual environments" – April 2014.

Prior Version

320. **What is the prior version of the Windows Server 2012 ADRMS External Connector license?**
Windows Server 2008 Rights Management Services External Connector license.

Reference: page 44, March 2016 Product Terms.

Windows Server 2008 RMS

Date Available

321. When was Windows Server 2008 RMS first available?

Windows Server 2008 RMS is a service of Windows Server 2008 which was first available in March 2008.

Reference: page 22, August 2009 Product List.

Licenses

322. What are the different licenses available for Windows Server 2008 RMS?
- Windows Server 2008 RMS CAL
- Windows Server 2008 RMS External Connector license

Reference: page 25, August 2012 Product List.

Licensing Model

323. How is Windows Server 2008 RMS licensed?

Windows Server RMS is a service of Windows Server 2008 and 2008 R2, so users or devices accessing RMS must first be licensed for access to the underlying Windows Server. Additionally, each user or device requires a Windows Server 2008 RMS CAL.

Reference: pages 30–31, 32, 33–34, & 35 April 2012 Product Use Rights.

Windows Server 2008 RMS

CALs

324. Which licenses, apart from RMS CALs, can be used to access Windows Server 2008 RMS?

The following license can be used as long as it had active SA on February 1, 2008, or was purchased after this date:
- Enterprise CAL Suite

Alternatively, any of the following licenses can be used as long as they had active SA on March 1, 2011, or were purchased after this date:
- Enterprise CAL Bridge for Office 365
- Enterprise CAL Bridge for Intune
- Enterprise CAL Bridge for Office 365 and Intune

Reference: pages 30–31, 32, 33–34, & 35 April 2012 Product Use Rights.

325. Can Windows Server 2008 RMS CALs be used to access RMS in Windows Server 2008 R2?

Yes.

Reference: pages 30–31, 32, 33–34, & 35 April 2012 Product Use Rights.

326. Are there Windows Server 2008 R2 RMS CALs?

No, the Windows Server 2008 RMS CALs were not updated when the Windows Server 2008 R2 licenses were released.

Reference: page 25, August 2012 Product List.

327. Can Windows Server 2008 RMS CALs be used to access RMS in any edition of Windows Server 2008 and 2008 R2 licensed with CALs?

Yes.

Reference: pages 30–31, 32, 33–34, & 35 April 2012 Product Use Rights.

Windows Server 2008 RMS

External Users

328. How are external users licensed for Windows Server 2008 RMS?
In addition to being licensed for Windows Server 2008, one of the following licenses is required:
- Windows Server 2008 RMS CAL, or
- Windows Server 2008 RMS External Connector license

Reference: pages 27–28, April 2012 Product Use Rights.

329. How is the Windows Server 2008 RMS External Connector license used?
One Windows Server 2008 RMS External Connector license must be assigned to each physical server accessed by external users. The server itself must be licensed in the usual way for Windows Server 2008 using Standard, Enterprise, Datacenter or Itanium Based Systems licenses. In addition, a Windows Server 2008 External Connector license must also be assigned to the server.

Reference: pages 31, 32, 34 & 35 April 2012 Product Use Rights.

330. Is there a Windows Server 2008 R2 RMS External Connector license?
No, the Windows Server 2008 RMS External Connector license was not updated when the Windows Server 2008 R2 licenses were released.

Reference: page 25, August 2012 Product List.

License Mobility

331. Do any of the Windows Server 2008 RMS licenses have License Mobility?
A Windows Server 2008 RMS External Connector license has License Mobility across Server Farm rights.

Reference: page 28, April 2012 Product Use Rights.

Windows Server 2008 RMS

New Version Rights

332. What are the new version rights for a Windows Server 2008 RMS External Connector license with SA?

For every license with active SA when Windows Server 2012 first became available in August 2012, or later:

- Windows Server 2012 ADRMS External Connector license

Reference: page 44, March 2016 Product Terms.

Prior Version

333. What is the prior version of the Windows Server 2008 RMS External Connector license?

Windows Rights Management Services 1.0 External Connector license.

Reference: page 21, January 2006 Product List.

Retired Licenses

334. Which Windows Server 2008 RMS licenses were retired when the 2012 version was introduced?

None.

Reference: page 44, March 2016 Product Terms.

Windows RMS 1.0

Licenses

335. What are the different licenses available for Windows Rights Management Services 1.0?
- Windows Rights Management Server CAL version 1.0
- Windows Rights Management Services 1.0 External Connector license

Reference: page 21, January 2006 Product List.

GLOSSARY

90-day rule
　Generally, a license may not be reassigned from one device or user more than once within a 90 day period.

　Reference: page 6, March 2016 Product Terms.

Additive CAL
　When there is a wide range of server functionality that CALs license access to there are often two levels of CALs with an Additive CAL licensing access to a more advanced set of functionality. The Additive CAL is always required in addition to a Base CAL. For example, a Windows Server 2012 CAL licenses access to the basic functionality of Windows Server 2012 R2 and an optional Windows Server 2012 RDS or RMS CAL may be licensed in addition to give access to further functionality in the Windows Server.

　Reference: page 70, March 2016 Product Terms.

Azure Hybrid Use Benefit
　This Software Assurance benefit, introduced in February 2016, allows a customer with Windows Server licenses covered with SA to procure an Azure virtual machine without Windows Server and then to assign an existing Windows Server license to it.

　Both Windows Server Standard and Datacenter licenses are eligible for this benefit, but the use rights differ: with Standard licenses it's an "alternative" right, which means that an organization can opt to use the license for either an on-premises server or for an Azure virtual machine, but not both. However, with Datacenter licenses it's an "additive" right which means that licenses can stay assigned to on-premises servers and also be assigned to an Azure virtual machine.

　Reference: pages 49–50, March 2016 Product Terms.

Glossary

BackOffice CAL
A single suite license consisting of Client Access License components for the following products:
- Windows 2000 Server
- SQL Server 2000
- Exchange Server 2000
- Systems Management Server 2.0
- Host Integration Server 2000
- Internet Security and Acceleration Server 2000

Reference: page 24, August 2001 Product List.

Base CAL
When there is a wide range of server functionality that CALs license access to there are often two levels of CALs with the Base CAL licensing access to the fundamental set of functionality. For example, a Windows Server 2012 CAL licenses access to the basic functionality of Windows Server 2012 R2 with optional Additive CALs licensing advanced functionality.

Reference: page 1, Volume Licensing Brief: "Base and Additive Client Access Licenses (CALs): An explanation" – August 2015.

Bridge CAL
Properly termed CAL Suite Bridges, these USLs are required when a CAL Suite licensed organization-wide is replaced with an Online Service. For example, an organization licensed with the Core CAL Suite which moves to Office 365 E1 needs the Core CAL Suite Bridge for Office 365 to continue to license the Windows Server CAL, System Center Configuration Manager CML and System Center Endpoint Protection components.

Reference: pages 14–15, March 2016 Product Terms.

Glossary

CAL (Client Access License)
CALs are assigned to users or devices which need to access the services of a server. A User CAL allows one licensed user access from any device, while a Device CAL allows any user access from the single licensed device.

Reference: page 70, March 2016 Product Terms.

CML (Client Management License)
CMLs allow organizations to use software such as the System Center products to manage an OSE on a device. A CML can be assigned to a user which allows the management of any OSEs on any devices used by that user. Alternatively, CMLs can be assigned to each OSE being managed.

Reference: page 10, March 2016 Product Terms.

Core CAL Suite
A single suite license, only available to be purchased with Software Assurance, which includes rights to the following licenses:
- Windows Server 2012 CAL
- System Center 2012 R2 Configuration Manager CML
- System Center 2012 R2 Endpoint Protection SL
- Exchange Server 2016 Standard CAL
- SharePoint Server 2013 Standard CAL
- Skype for Business Server 2015 Standard CAL

Reference: page 72, March 2016 Product Terms.

Date first available
This is the date that a product is first available, typically shown in Microsoft documentation as a month and year. It is the earlier of the date that Microsoft makes licenses available for ordering, or makes the software available to download from the Volume Licensing Service Center (VLSC).

Reference: page 69, March 2016 Product Terms.

Glossary

Down-edition rights
The rights to use a lower edition in place of a licensed higher-level edition. For example, Windows Server 2008 R2 Standard can be installed on a server to which a Windows Server 2008 R2 Datacenter edition license has been assigned.

Reference: page 6, March 2016 Product Terms.

Downgrade rights
The rights to use a previous version of the product in place of the licensed version. For example, Windows Server 2008 R2 Standard can be installed on a server to which a Windows Server 2012 R2 Standard edition license has been assigned.

Reference: page 6, March 2016 Product Terms.

Edition of a product
An edition is a way of differentiating between different features and functionality or different use rights that are included in a product. For example, Windows Server 2012 R2 Standard and Datacenter are different editions of Windows Server 2012 R2, and have different usage rights in virtualized environments.

Reference: Licensing School.

Enterprise Agreement
A Volume Licensing agreement for organizations with at least 250 devices or users. It requires an organization-wide commitment to one of the Enterprise Products (Windows, Office, and a CAL Suite) and Software Assurance is required on all license purchases. Perpetual licenses for on-premises products and subscription licenses for cloud services are available through this agreement.

More information: pages 8–14, Volume Licensing Guide.

Glossary

Enterprise CAL Suite
A single suite license, only available to be purchased with Software Assurance, which includes rights to the following licenses:
- Windows Server 2012 CAL
- Windows Server 2012 ADRMS CAL
- System Center 2012 R2 Configuration Manager CML
- System Center 2012 R2 Client Management Suite CML
- System Center 2012 R2 Endpoint Protection SL
- Exchange Server 2016 Standard CAL
- Exchange Server 2016 Enterprise CAL with Services
- SharePoint Server 2013 Standard CAL
- SharePoint Server 2013 Enterprise CAL
- Skype for Business Server 2015 Standard CAL
- Skype for Business Server 2015 Enterprise CAL
- Exchange Online Archiving for Exchange Server SL

Reference: page 72, March 2016 Product Terms.

Enterprise Mobility Suite
A single USL which includes rights to the following licenses:
- Azure Rights Management USL
- Microsoft Intune USL
- Azure Active Directory Premium USL
- Windows Server 2012 CAL
- Windows Server 2012 ADRMS CAL
- Advanced Threat Analytics CML
- System Center 2012 R2 Configuration Manager CML
- Microsoft Identity Manager CAL

Reference: page 72, March 2016 Product Terms, and page 26, March 2016 Online Services Terms.

Glossary

Enterprise Subscription Agreement
A Volume Licensing agreement for organizations with at least 250 devices or users. It requires an organization-wide commitment to one of the Enterprise Products (Windows, Office, and a CAL Suite) and Software Assurance is required on all license purchases. Subscription licenses for both on-premises products and cloud services are available through this agreement.

More information: pages 8–10, Volume Licensing Guide.

Extended Rights for RDS CALs
Organizations can use RDS User CALs with active Software Assurance to access Windows Server Azure virtual machines or Windows Server virtual machines running on the shared servers of a Service Provider. These rights first appeared in the January 2014 Product use Rights document.

Reference: pages 69–70, January 2014 Product Use Rights.

Extended support
The period after mainstream support which gives a reduced level of support. This typically lasts 5 years from the end of mainstream support and during this time Microsoft issues security updates only.

Reference: https://support.microsoft.com/en-us/lifecycle#gp/lifePolicy

External user
A user who is not an employee of the customer that owns the licenses, nor an employee of their affiliates or onsite contractors.

Reference: page 70, March 2016 Product Terms.

High Performance Computing (HPC)
High performance computing allows a computationally complex problem to be divided into a set of jobs and tasks that are solved in parallel across one or more computers.

Reference: page 70, March 2016 Product Terms.

Glossary

License
The rights to install software (where needed) and use it.
Reference: page 70, March 2016 Product Terms.

License Mobility across/within Server Farms
Note that this SA benefit confusingly changed its name from "License Mobility within Server Farms" to "License Mobility across Server Farms" with the launch of the July 2015 Product Terms document, but the rights remain the same, as described below.

When Server licenses have License Mobility across Server Farms rights they may be reassigned to any server within a server farm as often as needed without being restricted by the 90-day rule. This is important when virtual machines are moving between physical servers and need to remain appropriately licensed. Note that although licenses can be reassigned from one server farm to another, this can be no more frequently than every 90 days.

Reference: pages 82–83, March 2016 Product Terms.

License Mobility through Software Assurance
When Server licenses have License Mobility through Software Assurance rights they may be assigned to a Service Provider's shared hardware or to Azure, to license the server products in those environments. Windows Server licenses do not have these rights although the Azure Hybrid Use Benefit offers an alternative for licensing Azure virtual machines for Windows Server.

Reference: pages 82–83, March 2016 Product Terms.

Mainstream support
The period that a product is fully supported by Microsoft. This is typically 5 years, and during this time Microsoft supports requests to change product design and features as well as issuing security and non-security updates.

Reference: https://support.microsoft.com/en-us/lifecycle#gp/lifePolicy

Glossary

Microsoft Business Center (MBC)
A web portal used by customers with an MPSA in the US, Japan and Canada to download software, manage and activate SA benefits, and to view consolidated license and agreement information. Note that customers in the rest of the world will still use the MVLC until the MBC is rolled out to the rest of the world throughout 2016.

More information: https://businessaccount.microsoft.com/support

Microsoft Products and Services Agreement (MPSA)
A Volume Licensing agreement for organizations with at least 250 devices or users. It requires certain minimums to be met, but allows organizations to purchase licenses on an as-needed basis, with or without Software Assurance. Perpetual licenses for on-premises products and subscription licenses for cloud services are available through this agreement.

More information: pages 15–16, Volume Licensing Guide.

Microsoft Volume Licensing Center (MVLC)
A web portal used by customers with an MPSA to download software, manage and activate SA benefits, and to view consolidated license and agreement information. Note that customers in the US, Japan and Canada will use an updated version of this portal called the Microsoft Business Center from January 2016, and it will be rolled out to the rest of the world throughout 2016.

More information: https://businessaccount.microsoft.com/support

New version rights
One of the SA benefits for Windows Server licenses is the right to install a new version of a product if it becomes available during the period when SA is active.

Reference: page 75, March 2016 Product Terms.

Glossary

Online Services Terms

A document which is updated monthly and gives information on the use rights for the Microsoft Online Services.

Reference: page 4, March 2016 Product Terms.

Open agreement

A Volume Licensing agreement for organizations with less than 250 devices or users. A purchase of 5 licenses is typically required to start the agreement, and then organizations can purchase licenses on an as-needed basis, with or without Software Assurance. Perpetual licenses for on-premises products and subscription licenses for cloud services are available through this agreement.

More information: page 7, Volume Licensing Guide.

Open Value Company Wide agreement

A Volume Licensing agreement for organizations with less than 250 devices or users. It requires an organization-wide commitment to one of the Platform Products (Windows, Office, and a CAL Suite) for at least 5 devices, and Software Assurance is required on all license purchases. Perpetual licenses for on-premises products and subscription licenses for cloud services are available through this agreement.

More information: page 6, Volume Licensing Guide.

Open Value non-Company Wide agreement

A Volume Licensing agreement for organizations with less than 250 devices or users. A purchase of 5 licenses is typically required to start the agreement, and then organizations can purchase licenses on an as-needed basis. Software Assurance is required on all license purchases. Perpetual licenses for on-premises products and subscription licenses for cloud services are available through this agreement.

More information: page 6, Volume Licensing Guide.

Glossary

Open Value Subscription agreement

A Volume Licensing agreement for organizations with less than 250 devices or users. It requires an organization-wide commitment to one of the Platform Products (Windows, Office, and a CAL Suite) for at least 5 devices, and Software Assurance is required on all license purchases. Subscription licenses for both on-premises products and cloud services are available through this agreement.

More information: page 6, Volume Licensing Guide.

OSE (Operating System Environment)

An OSE is where an operating system is run. A server device with Windows Server 2012 R2 installed on the physical server and in four virtual machines running on the server has one physical OSE and four virtual OSEs.

Reference: page 71, March 2016 Product Terms.

Per Server mode

As a one-time alternative, rather than assigning CALs to users and devices, they can be assigned to a specific Windows Server virtual machine or physical server. For example, if an organization has 500 User CALs which they assign to a virtual machine, then any 500 users may concurrently access the Windows Server software on that specific virtual machine at any one time.

Reference: page 9, March 2016 Product Terms.

Perpetual license

A license that allows an organization to use the licensed software forever.

Reference: Licensing School.

Prior version

The version of a product immediately preceding another version. For example, the prior version of Windows Server 2012 R2 Standard is Windows Server 2012 Standard.

Reference: Licensing School.

Glossary

Processor-based/CAL licensing model
A Windows Server licensing model introduced with Windows Server 2012. Licenses are assigned to a server based on the number of physical processors in the server, with one license covering up to two processors. All processors in the server must be licensed, and a CAL is required for each user or device which accesses the server.

Note that when the Processor/CAL licensing model was retired (below), Microsoft started calling the new model the "Processor/CAL" model. We have kept the "Processor-based/CAL" name to differentiate between the models in different versions of Windows Server.

Reference: page 9, March 2016 Product Terms.

Processor/CAL licensing model
A Windows Server licensing model for some editions of Windows Server which ended with Windows Server 2008 R2. One license is assigned to the server for each physical processor in the server, and all processors much be licensed. A CAL is required for each user or device which accesses the server.

Reference: pages 27–28, April 2012 Product Use Rights.

Product List document
A document which was updated monthly and gave information on Microsoft product availability. This document was replaced by the Product Terms document in July 2015.

Reference: page 4, March 2016 Product Terms.

Product Terms document
A document which is updated monthly and gives information on the availability of Microsoft products and their associated use rights. This document is the successor to the Product List and Product Use Rights documents starting from July 2015.

Reference: page 4, March 2016 Product Terms.

Glossary

Product Use Rights document
A document which was updated quarterly and gave information on the use rights associated with Microsoft products. This document was replaced by the Product Terms document in July 2015.
Reference: page 4, March 2016 Product Terms.

Select Plus agreement
A Volume Licensing agreement for organizations with at least 250 devices or users. It requires certain minimums to be met, but allows organizations to purchase licenses on an as-needed basis, with or without Software Assurance. Perpetual licenses for on-premises products and subscription licenses for cloud services are available through this agreement. Select Plus is being retired and no new Select Plus agreements have been signed after July 1, 2015.
More information: pages 16–18, Volume Licensing Guide.

Server/CAL licensing model
A Windows Server licensing model for some editions of Windows Server which ended with Windows Server 2008 R2. A single license is assigned to the server and a CAL is required for each user or device which accesses the server.
Reference: pages 27–28, April 2012 Product Use Rights.

Server farm
A single data center or two data centers, each physically located either in time zones not more than four hours apart, or within the European Union or European Free Trade Association.
Reference: page 71, March 2016 Product Terms.

Server licensing model
A Windows Server licensing model for some editions of Windows Server which ended with Windows Server 2008 R2. A single license is assigned to the server and no CALs are required for users or devices which access the server.
Reference: page 71, April 2012 Product Use Rights.

Glossary

SL (Subscription License)
A license that allows software to be used for a defined period of time – during the term of a Volume Licensing agreement, for example.

Reference: page 71, March 2016 Product Terms.

Software Assurance (SA)
A collection of benefits to help organizations deploy, manage and use Microsoft products. SA can be added to a license purchase, typically for a three-year term. At the agreement renewal the SA can be renewed without having to purchase the license again.

Reference: pages 48–51, Volume Licensing Guide.

Step-Up license
If a license for a lower edition of a product has been purchased with Software Assurance, it can be stepped up to the higher edition license. For example, a Step-Up license can be purchased for a Windows Server 2012 R2 Standard license to give rights to the Datacenter edition.

Reference: page 81, March 2016 Product Terms.

Suite license
A product that is comprised of components that are also licensed separately. A suite is a single license that is assigned to a single user or device, and the components may not be separated and used on separate devices or by separate users.

Reference: page 69, March 2016 Product Terms.

USL or User SL (User Subscription License)
A non-perpetual license assigned to a specific user, typically used to give access to Online Services.

Reference: page 4, March 2016 Online Services Terms.

Glossary

Version of a product
A particular release of Windows Server often corresponding to a year – Windows Server 2012, for example.

Reference: Licensing School.

VDI Suite
A subscription license assigned to a device licensing it for Windows Server Remote Desktop Services for use in a Virtual Desktop Infrastructure (VDI) environment, and System Center Virtual Machine Manager.

Reference: pages 62–63, April 2015 Product Use Rights.

Volume Licensing Service Center (VLSC)
A web portal used by Volume Licensing customers with all agreements except the MPSA to download software, manage and activate SA benefits, and to view consolidated license and agreement information. MPSA customers use the Microsoft Volume Licensing Center (MLVC).

More information: https://www.microsoft.com/Licensing/servicecenter

Web Workload
Web pages, websites, web applications and web services which are publicly available and not limited to an organization's employees or affiliates.

Reference: page 71, March 2016 Product Terms.

INDEX

GETTING THE MOST FROM THIS BOOK 1
WINDOWS SERVER 5
   General Licensing Questions 5
      CALs 5
      Downgrade Rights 8
      External Connector License 6
      Fail-Over Licensing 9
      License Reassignment 8
      Software Assurance 7
      Storage Server 9
      Virtualization Licensing 8
   Windows Server 2012 R2 10
      CALs 11
      Date Available 10
      Down-Edition Rights 15
      External Users 13
      License Mobility 16
      Licenses 10
      Licensing Models 10
      Mainstream and Extended Support Dates 17
      Microsoft Identity Manager 2016 12
      Per Server Mode 13
      Prior Versions 16
      Step-Up Licenses 16
      Virtualization Licensing 14
   Windows Server 2012 18
      CALs 19
      Date Available 18
      Down-Edition Rights 22
      External Users 20
      License Mobility 23
      Licenses 18

Licensing Models 18
Mainstream and Extended Support Dates..24
New Version Rights..23
Per Server Mode 20
Prior Versions 24
Retired Editions 24
Step-Up Licenses..23
Virtualization Licensing 21
Windows Server 2008 R2 25
   CALs...27
   Date Available 25
   Down-Edition Rights 32
   External Users...29
   License Mobility..33
   Licenses 25
   Licensing Models 25
   Mainstream and Extended Support Dates.....................................38
   New Version Rights...34
   Per Server Mode 28
   Prior Versions 37
   Retired Editions 39
   Step-Up Licenses...34
   Virtualization Licensing 30
Windows Server 2008 40
   CALs...42
   Date Available 40
   Down-Edition Rights 47
   External Users...43
   License Mobility..48
   Licenses 40
   Licensing Models 41
   Mainstream and Extended Support Dates.....................................52
   New Version Rights...49
   Per Server Mode 43
   Prior Versions 51

Index

Retired Editions 52
Step-Up Licenses 48
Virtualization Licensing 45
Windows Server 2003 R2 53
   Licenses 53
   Mainstream and Extended Support Dates 53
Windows Server 2003 55
   Datacenter Edition 55
   Licenses 55
   Mainstream and Extended Support Dates 55
Windows Server 2000 56
   Datacenter Server 56
   Licenses 56
   Mainstream and Extended Support Dates 56
Licensing Windows Server in Microsoft Azure 57
   Azure Windows Server Virtual Machines 57
   Using Windows Server Datacenter Licenses 58
   Using Windows Server Standard Licenses 57

REMOTE DESKTOP SERVICES 60
General Licensing Questions 60
   Anonymous Use 64
   Application Virtualization for Remote Desktop Services ... 63
   Availability 60
   CALs 60
   External Connector License 63
   Terminal Services 60
Windows Server 2012 RDS 65
   CALs 65
   Date Available 65
   External Users 67
   License Mobility 67
   Licenses 65
   Licensing Model 65
   Prior Version 68
   USL 66

- Windows Server 2008 RDS 69
  - CALs 69
  - Date Available 69
  - External Users 70
  - License Mobility 71
  - Licenses 69
  - Licensing Model 69
  - New Version Rights 72
  - Prior Version 72
  - Retired Licenses 72
- Windows Server 2008 Terminal Services 73
  - CALs 73
  - Date Available 73
  - External Users 74
  - License Mobility 74
  - Licenses 73
  - Licensing Model 73
  - New Version Rights 75
  - Prior Version 75
  - Retired Licenses 75
- Windows Server 2003 Terminal Services 76
  - Licenses 76
- Windows Server 2000 Terminal Services 77
  - Licenses 77

ACTIVE DIRECTORY RIGHTS MANAGEMENT SERVICES 79
- General Licensing Questions 79
  - Availability 79
  - CALs 79
  - External Connector License 80
- Windows Server 2012 ADRMS 81
  - CALs 82
  - Date Available 81
  - External Users 83
  - License Mobility 84
  - Licenses 81

  Licensing Model 81
  Prior Version 84
  USL 83
 Windows Server 2008 RMS 85
  CALs 86
  Date Available 85
  External Users 87
  License Mobility 87
  Licenses 85
  Licensing Model 85
  New Version Rights 88
  Prior Version 88
  Retired Licenses 88
 Windows RMS 1.0 89
  Licenses 89
GLOSSARY 91